The Digital Imaging Dictionary

JOE FARACE

ALLWORTH PRESS

DEDICATION

This book is dedicated to my father, Joe Farace Sr., and the memory of my mother, Delores Farace. By giving me my first camera when I was eight years old and my first good 35 mm camera when I was a teenager, both of them inspired me to pursue a career in photography. All through my life they have encouraged me—and all of their children—to think for themselves and always strive for excellence. For that I will forever be grateful.

Published by Allworth Press
an imprint of Allworth Communications, Inc.
10 East 23rd Street, New York, NY 10010

Cover design by Douglas Design Associates, New York, NY
Book design by Sharp Des!gns, Holt, MI

ISBN: 1-880559-46-3
Library of Congress Catalog Card Number: 96-83242

contents

acknowledgments

This book began with a story I originally wrote for *Shutterbug* magazine in 1995. In an article on computer basics for photographers, I created what I then called "A Shutterbug's Dictionary of Computer Terms." The original *Shutterbug* story was commissioned by Associate Editor, Tony Galluzzo, who asked me to write a story about bits and bytes and how they affected today's photography. It was this story that got me to thinking about creating a digital imaging dictionary. While this brief magazine article may have been my first effort at trying to pull together digital imaging terms and definitions, it was Allworth Press' Tad Crawford and Ted Gachot's original idea to create this book. They were kind enough to ask me to write it. Many thanks to them.

A book like this cannot be assembled without the assistance of many. Here are some additional people that I would like to thank.

The publisher asked me to find someone to give the book a "good technical read" before submission, and I was lucky to have Vern Prime offer to do that. Vern is an experienced camera repair person as well as the most technically knowledgeable person about IBM-PC and compatible computers that I've ever met. I am lucky to have a Prime-built PC in my office for use with Windows-based digital imaging tools—and to have Vern as a friend.

All photographs, unless otherwise indicated, were provided by the manufacturers. The photographic print images in this book were digitized with an Epson 1000 flatbed scanner that was generously loaned to me for this project by Epson America. I am grateful for their assistance with this book, particularly from Epson's Nancy Napurski, who has been a great help to me with this and other digital imaging projects. Illustrations from slides were scanned on a Nikon Coolscan, and I want to thank P. Plitteris of Nikon Technical Support for help in sorting out some early software conflicts I encountered. I would also like to thank Sonya Schaefer of Adobe Systems for keeping me up to date with the latest developments in Adobe Photoshop, Photo Deluxe, Gallery Effects, and other products. Another big thank-you goes out to Kristen Keyes of MetaTools, the creators of Kai's Power Tools plug-ins, for making sure I had information about and review copies of their latest products. Chip Partner of Saphar Associates and Terry McCardle of Eastman Kodak kept me current with the up-to-the-minute data of Kodak's digital cameras, Photo CD, and Advance Photo System digitizing system. I appreciate their assistance.

There are also two special people I would like to thank, without whose encouragement and nurturing I would never even have been asked to write this book. Fred Schmidt was editor of *Photomethods* magazine when he "discovered" me while I was presenting a seminar on photography. Fred, along with his associate editor Elinor Stecker-Orel, now contributing editor to *Popular Photography*, had faith in my abilities, and for that I will always be grateful.

There are many photographers and computer users who have helped me over the years. Without their assistance this book would have been more difficult. That's why I would like to thank Don and Linda Feltner for their help, guidance, and inspiration for fifteen years. I was a fan of Don Feltner's for many years before he became my friend. I'm still a big fan. I have also appreciated the technical assistance of Mike Phelps and Brad Tombaugh, the original sparkplugs for the Macintech user's group.

Their knowledge and willingness to share that knowledge was a big help to me and I will always be grateful.

Lastly, I would like to thank my wife, Mary, for her encouragement in this and other book projects, my fine arts photography, as well as my life. I would not be half the writer, photographer, and human being I am without her love and support.

All of these wonderful folks are responsible for the good things you will find between the covers of this book. Any mistakes, errors, or omissions you discover are all mine.

JOE FARACE
Denver, Colorado, 1995

introduction

As digital imaging comes into wider usage, we are gradually moving this medium [motion pictures] *away from a purely photographic interpretation of reality into one that is more painterly.*

GEORGE LUCAS

Reality is what's left after the movie stops.

PHILIP K. DICK

Buzzwords

Like other technical and artistic disciplines, photography has more than its share of jargon. As photographers we "shoot" brides and kids, "bracket" our shots, and apply "Zone IV" interpretations to an image on "sheet" film that's processed using "N+1" development. Yet surprisingly, when digital photography became practical, we couldn't even agree on a name for it. Was it digital imaging, digital photography, or as one pundit put it, "pixography"?

What is digital imaging anyway? Here's my definition and one that will be used throughout this book: Digital imaging is a process that converts photographic images into their mathematical equivalents, much as conventional chemical-based methods turn silver grains into photographs.

It may come as a surprise to you that many of the principles surrounding digital imaging are not new. They are an outgrowth of all that has gone before in the computer processing of text, along with advances in desktop publishing and prepress applications. Digital imaging is nothing more than the next, logical extension of the kind of camera and darkroom techniques photographers have been using for over a century. The tools used may appear to be different, but they are no more of a radical change than late-nineteenth-century daguerreotypists encountered when they switched from dipping their silver-plated copper sheets into mercury vapor to using glass-plate negatives coated with albumen.

Three Little Words

The digital imaging process consists of three major aspects: acquisition, enhancement, and output.

I. Acquisition

When becoming involved with digital imaging, one of the first things you may notice is that digital photographers don't "shoot" photographs, they "acquire" images. There are several ways this can be accomplished.

Making a photograph with a digital camera is one of the easiest ways to produce or acquire an image in digital form. Another way to acquire digital images is to shoot photographs with print or slide film, then use a *scanner* to *digitize* the images. Scanners are computer accessories (**peripherals**) that convert the original text, graphics, or photographs into a digital form. They accomplish this by passing a light-emitting element across the original image, transforming it into a group of electronic signals that is ultimately stored as a digital file. My favorite method of acquiring digital images is the Kodak Photo CD process, which uses a proprietary scanning and storage system to digitize and store images made with slide and negative film in formats from 35 mm to 4×5 sheet film.

II. Enhancement

Of the three aspects of digital photography, image enhancement has generated the most interest and excitement. I think this is because it was put to effective use by early adopters of the technology to create photographic images that could never have been created using any other means. This created hype surrounding image enhancement software, but digital imaging is like a tripod; you need all three legs to support it.

Nevertheless, image enhancement is important. You can use enhancement and manipulation techniques to improve and change images much as you would in a traditional darkroom. No matter what software tool you use for digital image enhancement, they all do the same thing: manipulate an image in some manner to achieve a desired effect, much the way a photographer working in a darkroom manipulates the silver grains in film and paper. Among the many advantages of a digital darkroom is that you don't have to work in the dark or get your hands wet—and there are no annoying smells to deal with. And more often than not, achieving dramatic effects is easier to accomplish digitally than working with paper and chemistry.

III. Output

Because of the high cost of the original photographic-quality printers and film recorders, image output is one of the least talked-about of the three elements that make up the digital imaging process. All that is changing as new low-cost dye-sublimation and inkjet printers are making it possible for even amateur pixographers to produce photo-realistic output on their desktop. Now, there's plenty to talk about.

Output can appear in many different forms. On a basic level, digital photographs can be viewed on a monitor. In this way, Kodak's Photo CD process can be used as a method for both outputting images as well as acquiring them. You can, for example, digitize and store your images on a Photo CD disc, then take that disc to a friend's house and use a Photo CD player to display your photographs on their television set. Used in this way, the Photo CD player becomes a kind of electronic slide projector.

You can also attach a printer to your computer to reproduce photographs in grayscale or color. The quality of this output can be impressive—especially considering the reasonable cost of the latest generation of inexpensive color printers from companies like Epson and Fargo.

Another output option is to have your images converted back into silver-based form. Service bureaus and professional photo labs have equipment called film recorders that can take your enhanced image in digital form and turn it into a 35 mm slide or a sheet of 4×5 and 8×10

negative or transparency film. Once the image is back in silver-based form, you can project it or use it to make prints in the traditional manner.

If any or all of this seems unfamiliar to you, don't despair. Many of the most commonly used terms, acronyms, and buzzwords that are part of the digital imaging process are explained and defined in the pages of this book.

Learning a New Language

When photographers began creating images in purely digital form and started converting silver-based images into digital ones, a whole new set of buzzwords entered the vernacular. As you will discover by browsing though this book, digital imaging uses terms that originated in many places, including conventional photography, the printing and prepress industry, and the world of microcomputers. Navigating though these buzzwords, while trying to understand what's going on, can be a daunting prospect for newcomers. The purpose of this book is to provide a desktop reference source for photographers, printers, graphic designers, prepress workers, art directors, and other communications professionals that have to work—or want to work—with digital images but may lack the technical background or experience to understand the language of computing and imaging.

In compiling this dictionary, I have tried to provide common-sense, conversational definitions for the typical buzzwords you might encounter when working with digital images or digital imaging techniques. In writing the definitions, I've assumed that you are already involved in photography or the visual arts but may not be as computer literate as you might like. That's why you will find many words that deal with computing and computers. Just as it is impossible to write about the technical side of photography without mentioning optics and chemistry, it's difficult to separate the technology of computing from the digital imaging process. So you'll find plenty of computer buzzwords as well as words strictly related to the creation of digital images and graphics.

What's in this Book and Why

Unlike some other books on digital imaging, this one was *not* designed to be read cover-to-cover, although you may feel free to do so if you like. Instead, *The Digital Imaging Dictionary* has been designed to sit next to your computer and help you interpret software and hardware reviews, read a program's user's guide or manual, or successfully communicate with your service bureau. And unlike many other dictionaries, this one includes opinions, personal experiences, and tips on how to avoid problems or overcome the occasional digital dilemma. I consider this additional information to be part of an extended definition of what a term or buzzword means. All of the stories are true, and the advice—like any found in any computer book—must be balanced against your own experiences in computing and digital imaging in order to be applied to your specific situation. Consider the tips you find here to be a starting point for your own digital explorations. All the advice is offered with the best of intentions—to keep you from making some of the same mistakes that I've made.

Because some definitions may contain technical words that you may not know, you'll also find plenty of cross-references to make this book as user-friendly as I could make it. When a definition includes buzzwords that are defined elsewhere in *The Digital Imaging Dictionary*, those words appear in **bold type** so you'll be able to look elsewhere for a complete definition. Sometimes, a definition of a term has been included in another definition. This was done to keep you from bouncing back and forth within the book when all you are doing is looking for a simple answer to (what you think may be) a simple question.

Definitions are as cross-platform as I could make them. When I provide an explanation of a term like **buffer**, I make sure that it is the same for either Microsoft Windows or Macintosh users. If not, such as is the case for **dialog box**, I provide information for both Mac and Windows applications. And you'll find there are some definitions, like the Macintosh PDS (Processor Direct Slot) for example, that are not applicable in a IBM-PC or compatible environment. Whenever a term is platform-specific, I make sure to call the reader's attention to it. If I don't mention that a definition is for a Macintosh or Windows-using computer *only*, you can safely assume that it is common to both platforms.

Many times it is not enough to know exactly what a term means. A strict definition of a term or acronym may tell you what it is but not what it does, or why it's important to digital imaging. That's why, many times, a definition will include detailed description of how an individual component fits into the digital imaging puzzle. There will also be some definitions that include a how-to section explaining how the item you are looking up works and providing tips on using the technique or hardware.

Some definitions include mini-reviews or roundups of products in a specific category, such as image database programs. Then there are definitions, such as the one for **fonts**, that include what I feel is "everything you ever wanted to know" about the subject.

In the real world you'll encounter words that have more than one meaning, and the world of digital imaging and computers is no exception. When you find a word that has more than one definition, I've numbered the different explanations and placed them in sequence, with the first being the most common, followed by secondary usages in decreasing order of their popularity. This is the case, for example, with the word **clone**. The term refers both to a type of computer and to a tool found in many image-manipulation programs. In *The Digital Imaging Dictionary,* you'll find explanations of both usages.

Some definitions include explanatory text that will provide additional information to expand your knowledge of the term. For example, the definition for bit depth includes not only what "bit depth" means but also information about the different kinds you're likely to encounter in looking at computer hardware and what the significance of these differences are to digital photographers. There are also some definitions that contain a brief history lesson so that you will learn—if you want to—where certain products, techniques, or terms originated. In general, these little side trips of trivia or extra detail will appear as separate paragraphs following the main definition, so you can ignore them if "all you want are the facts."

I tried not to be repetitive but, at the same time, I wanted to keep readers from Ping-Ponging back and forth around the book. This means there is some repetition but, with my editor's help, I have tried to keep duplication to a minimum. I've also tried to be as thorough as I could. But no matter how hard I've tried, there are sure to be some omissions as well as the inevitable additions that will appear as new digital imaging hardware and techniques come into wider use. If you see a glaring omission, please drop me a note, care of the publisher, or send me electronic mail at 75300.413@compuserve.com. I will see to it that your addition or correction is included in the next edition of *The Digital Imaging Dictionary,* and that you are credited for its inclusion.

If you don't already have a computer, flip to Appendix A and take a look at a basic checklist that will help you determine the kind of system you'll need for digital imaging. Taking a few minutes to ask yourself a few questions about the imaging work you do—or plan on doing—will save you time and money when you make your purchase or upgrade.

Lastly, you will encounter those occasions when a definition refers to specific product and manufacturer. To make it possible for readers to contact the companies mentioned in the book, I've included their name, address, phone, and fax information in Appendix B.

TECHNICAL NOTE

A technical note for those readers who are interested in that sort of thing: This book was written using a Power Macintosh 8100/80 using Microsoft Word 6.01, and some final editing was done on an Apple PowerBook 180 laptop computer using the same word processing program. The original manuscript was printed on an Epson Stylus Color printer, but a copy was provided to the publisher on floppy disk. Print images were scanned on an Epson EC1000 flatbed scanner and 35 mm slides were scanned using Nikon's Coolscan film scanner. When necessary, both kinds of images were converted into black-and-white images and tweaked with Adobe Photoshop before placement in the final manuscript by the designer. Digital images for all of the illustrations were provided to the book's designer on a 44MB SyQuest cartridge.

After translating files from IBM to Macintosh format using MacLink Plus, the text was cleaned up and massaged using Microsoft Word 5.0. Design and layout was done on a Power Macintosh 8100/100 with 106 megs of RAM using Adobe Page-Maker 6.01 with the help of PageTools 2.0 from Extensis. Text is set in Adobe Concorde and Avenir fonts, while the section heads are set in Image Club's Rubino typeface. Laser galleys were printed on an NEC Silentwriter 2, and the layout was provided to the printer on a 44MB SyQuest cartridge for final output.

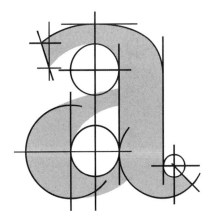

access arm On any magnetic storage disk (**hard disk** or **removable media**) drive, this is the part of the hardware that holds the read/write heads that read or write data on the disk.

access bus This is a **bus** standard that provides two-way communications between peripherals and the **CPU**. Bus slots accept printed circuit cards that allow accessories or devices to be attached to the computer's motherboard. The use of the ACCESS bus standard eliminates the need for the user to install complex files or **drivers**. For more detailed information, see **expansion bus** and **expansion slot**.

access time The performance of fixed or removable drives is measured by **seek time**, or the amount of time required for the arm of a direct access storage device to position itself over the appropriate track.

ADP Automatic Data Processing.

advanced photo system Sometimes erroneously called APS. (APS is a registered trademark of Alliance Peripheral Systems of Kansas City, a manufacturer or **hard disks** and **removable media** drives.) This is a new cartridge-based film format that was developed by an international consortium that included Canon, Fuji, Kodak, Nikon, and Minolta. The film cartridge (called *Advantix* by Kodak and *Fujicolor Smart Film* by Fuji) features a drop-in loading system that means that a photographer will never have to touch the film. The film is returned after processing rolled back into the original cartridge. The film itself measures 25 mm wide instead of 35 mm and features a full-frame image size of 16.7 × 30.2 mm, compared to 24 × 36 mm for standard 35 mm film. It also has sprocket holes on one side, instead of both sides as is typical for 35 mm film. The other edge is coated with a magnetic stripe that allows an Advanced Photo System camera to shoot three different formats—at the flick of a switch:

- full frame (16.7 × 30.2 mm)
- AL (15.6 × 22.3 mm)
- Panoramic (9.6 × 27.4 mm)

The Advanced Photo System processing equipment can read the data encoded onto the magnetic strip and produce prints in three different sizes from a single roll (cassette) of film.

What does this film format mean to the digital imager? One of the first new digital products that will utilize Advanced Photo Systems film is Kodak's new **Picture Disk** service. Picture Disk is both software and digitizing service that will place up to twenty-eight image files on a floppy disk. For more details on this new service, see **Picture Disk**.

At the 1996 Photo Marketing Association's Trade Show, Fuji Photo Film introduced a new processing system that, in addition to making prints, would return digitized images from Advanced Photo System film on **floppy disk**, **CD-ROM**, and **Zip** data cartridges. They will also be offering a drop-in loading film digitizer (for under $500) that can be connected to your home or office computer and will scan and digitize images made on Fujicolor Smart Film. Is this a challenge to Kodak's Photo CD?

At this point it is hard to say. Some industry pundits have called Advanced Photo System "a cure for no known disease" and point at the failure of other smaller format systems such as 126 Instamatic and disc film. Others hail it as a blending of silver-based technology with digital. One thing's for sure; Advanced Photo System is being launched with as much hype as Windows 95 was.

Will Advanced Photo System have an expanded section in the next edition of this dictionary or will it be a curious, historical footnote? Stay tuned.

AI Artificial Intelligence.

algorithm In basic mathematical terms, a set of defined rules (or part of a **program**) that solves a problem.

alias A feature of the Macintosh operating system which allows users to create a small file that acts as a substitute (or pointer) which, when double clicked, launches the original application or document. This allows users to keep original files buried deep in folders, or even to store them on removable media or a network, and get to them without a lot of muss or fuss. In Windows 95, the alias concept is implemented as a "shortcut." Do not confuse alias with **aliasing**, below.

aliasing Sometimes when a graphic is displayed on a monitor, you'll see jagged edges around some objects. These rough edges are caused by an effect called *aliasing*. Techniques that smooth out the "jaggies" are called *anti-aliasing*. Do not confuse aliasing with **alias**, above.

alpha version This is the version of new software that precedes beta and is typically only used within the environment in which it was created, i.e. is rarely used outside the developer's company.

AMCOMEX American Computer Exchange is an organization that tracks and publishes the street prices of used Macintosh computers. Like the so-called "blue book" used by car dealers, there are price guides available to help the used-computer shopper find out what specific used Macintosh models cost. Magazines, like *MacWorld*, print the American Computer Exchange used-computer prices in the back of each issue. You'll also find listings from the National Computer Exchange (**NACOMEX**) in publications like *ComputerUSER*. You can safely use these prices as a guide to what you should pay for the used computer of your choice.

analog Information presented in continuous form, corresponding to a representation of the "real world." A traditional photographic print is an analog form, but when this same image is scanned, it is broken into digital form, made up of bits of information.

ANSI The American National Standards Institute is an organization that determines and distributes data processing standards that may be adopted on a voluntary basis by the industry. ANSI is the U.S. member of the **ISO**.

apps Shorthand for applications. Adobe Photoshop and PageMaker may properly be called *applications*, but are often called just *apps*.

ASCII American Standard Code for Information Interchange. ASCII is a standardized computer code for representing text data. The code has ninety-six displayed characters (characters you can see on the screen) and thirty-two non-displayed characters (some of which you can see, others that you can't).

ASMP The American Society of Media Photographers was founded in 1944 by a handful of the world's leading photojournalists. Within a few years, standards were established and speculative shooting was replaced with guarantees. Credit lines appeared more regularly and photographers began to retain ownership of their images. Growth continued from the original eight founders to more than five thousand members today. ASMP seeks:

- To protect and promote the interests of photographers whose work is for publication.
- To promote high professional standards and ethics.
- To cultivate friendship and mutual understanding between photographers.

Further information may be obtained by writing or calling ASMP National 609/799.8300 voice, 609/799.2233 fax, 14 Washington Park, Suite 502, Princeton Junction, NJ 08550-1033. (Information courtesy ASMP online membership brochure.)

asynchronous This is a common form of two-way data transmission in which each character is transmitted as a discrete unit having its own start and stop characters. This allows for the sending and receiving units (or **modems**) *not* to be in synchronization.

ATM Adobe Type Manager. Since not all printers can handle **PostScript** fonts, Adobe developed ATM, which lets you print PostScript fonts on non-PostScript printers. For details, see **fonts**.

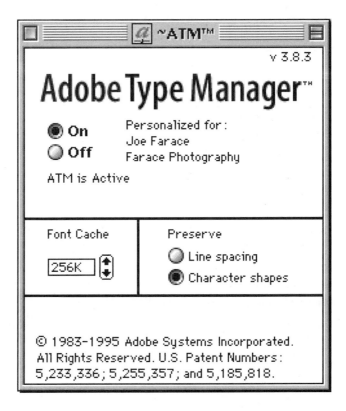

One of the most useful utilities for either Windows or Macintosh computers is Adobe Systems Adobe Type Manager. It allows the use of high-quality PostScript fonts to print on non-PostScript printers.

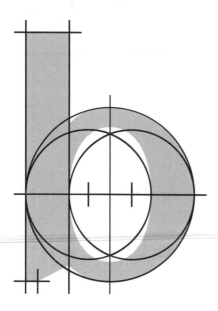

backslash This is the character "\" which is part of the standard **ASCII** character set but isn't found on a conventional typewriter. This character is oh-so-familiar to users of Microsoft's MS-DOS or Windows, although Windows 95 users will not encounter it as much. The key is also on all Macintosh keyboards, but most Mac-heads will never use it.

backup A duplicate copy of data stored on media other than the original, used to reconstruct the data in case of hardware or software problems. Sometimes backups can be stored on **floppy disk** or some other form of **removable media**. One of the oldest rules in computing is backup, backup, backup.

backward compatible Hardware or software that is compatible with any earlier version of a similar product. For example: A 1.44MB floppy disk on a Macintosh is backward compatible and is able to read 800K disks.

Adobe PageMaker 6.0 is backward compatible with files created with version 5.0.

BASIC Beginners All-purpose Symbolic Instruction Code. A programming language that was developed in the mid 1960s by John Kemeny and Thomas Kurtz at Dartmouth College. BASIC is considered one of the easiest programming languages to learn and simple programs can be quickly written by new programmers with a minimum of instruction or practice.

batch processing The collection of data or images into a group, or *batch* to be processed by the computer at the same time.

baud Used as a measure of speed in data transmission, synonymous with *bits per second.*

BBS A Bulletin Board System that can be accessed by a **modem**. Many computer companies like Epson and Fargo operate BBSs so that customers can download the latest software—especially **drivers** for graphics cards, monitors, and printers—directly from the manufacturer.

Bernoulli box One of the most interesting removable magnetic drives is the Bernoulli box. The name comes from an eighteenth-century Swiss scientist named Daniel Bernoulli, who originally demonstrated the principles of fluid dynamics. A Bernoulli box uses a combination of both floppy and hard disk technologies. Unlike a traditional hard disk in which a read/write head floats over a rigid disk, the Bernoulli disk is flexible (it's made of material similar to floppy disks) and bends at high speeds to be close enough for the head to read it. During a power failure, a hard disk must retract its head to prevent a crash, whereas the Bernoulli floppy naturally bends away. Bernoulli drives are made exclusively by Iomega Corporation.

beta testing The way in which software is tested with "real world" data outside the manufacturer's environment. This software is usually called *beta* or *prerelease* software and is given to the press and selected users to try before final release of the "shrink-wrapped" version. Beta testers are expected to report problems back to the manufacturer so they can be fixed before final release. The software that precedes beta is called **alpha** and typically is only used within the environment in which it was created.

binary A mathematical system based on the numbers one and zero. This is ideal for computers, because electrical signals can be represented by electrical current being positive and negative, on and off.

BIOS Basic Input/Output Systems. This computer chip is part of a **motherboard**, an auxiliary card, that controls the input and output devices connected to it.

bit *Bi*nary dig*it*. The smallest unit of information a computer can work with. Because they represent all data (including photographs) by using numbers, or *digits*, computers are digital devices. These digits are measured in bits. (See **binary** above.) Each electronic signal therefore becomes one bit, but to represent more complex numbers or images, computers must combine these signals into larger 8-bit groups called *bytes*. When 1,024 (not one thousand) bytes are combined, you get a **kilobyte**, often called just plain *K*. When you lasso 1,024 kilobytes, you have a **megabyte** (MB) or "meg."

bit depth This specification refers to the number of bits that are assigned to each **pixel**. The more bits you have, the more photo-realistic the screen image. Let's look at the typical choices in bit depth for computer screens:
- *1-bit*: If a computer has the ability to display 1-bit per pixel, each pixel can either be black or white. This is called a monochrome system, and these monitors are usually sharper and emit less radiation than color models.
- *4-bit*: Some computers, especially laptops, offer 4-bit video capability, which translates into sixteen shades of gray or color.
- *8-bit*: essentially the standard display for today's computers. With an 8-bit color depth, you can see 256 colors or levels of gray. An 8-bit system can work well for black-and-white photographs, but is just barely adequate for critical evaluation of a color photograph. Images on an 8-bit system will not be displayed 100 percent accurately and photographs will look posterized and consequently less realistic.
- *16-bit*: Fast becoming a new minimum standard, it has the potential to display 32,000 different colors. At 16-bits and above, the video

signal must split into thirds, providing one each for the red, blue, and green channels. Your computer devotes 15 bits to color (5 bits per color channel), and the one remaining bit is used to overlay all these colors. In practice, you get 32,768 colors, and when fewer colors are displayed, another color is substituted for the "correct" one. This shows up on screen as a slightly posterized image.

- *24-bit*: Each pixel on a screen can handle up to 256 colors, which lets systems display 16.7 million colors. A 24-bit model provides true photographic quality.
- *32-bit*: Often when someone is talking about 32-bit color, they really mean 24-bit. Only a few computers offer 32-bit capabilities. Typically they allocate one byte (8 bits) for each of the primary colors and the final byte to display images from sources such as videotape. The additional byte adds functionality but not more colors.

Since 256 levels of gray are displayed on an 8-bit system, that's all you really need when working with black-and-white digital photographs, but if you plan on working with color images, you should use a computer that has a 24-bit display. Some devices, including digital cameras, are capable of higher color depths up to 42 bits (14 bits per pixel) for greater color fidelity, and these will be covered in Section C.

bit resolution Often called *color depth*, it measures the number of bits of information a pixel can store and determines how many colors can be displayed at once.

bitmap Graphic files come in three classes: bitmap, **metafile**, and **vector**. A bitmap (formerly known as **raster**) is any graphic image that is composed of a collection of tiny individual dots or pixels—one for every point or dot on a computer screen. The simplest bitmapped files are **monochrome** images composed of only black and white pixels.

Monochrome bitmaps have a single color against a background while images displaying more shades of color or gray need more than one bit to define the colors. Images, like photographs, with many different levels of color or gray are called *deep bitmap*, while black-and-white graphics are called *bi-level bitmap*. A bitmap's depth is permanently fixed at creation. The screen shots that accompany this dictionary have a resolution of 72 dpi (dots per inch). No matter what I do, I can't change this. I can make them bigger, but not better.

BMP (Windows) Often pronounced "bump." This acronym is a file **extension** for a specific kind of Windows-based bitmap graphics file. Digital photographs may be saved as a BMP or any other kind of bitmapped file format.

bomb Can be a verb or noun, but the result is always the same–an abrupt halt, **crash**, or lack of functioning. *Bomb* usually refers to a program or system (software) failure. In the Macintosh operating system, bombs may be accompanied by a dialog box containing a graphic bomb–like you didn't already know you had problems.

boot To load your computer's operating system into memory so it can begin functioning. This is sometimes called a "cold boot," to differentiate it from a "warm boot" or restart that has been performed after your computer has been running for a while.

BPS Bits Per Second, sometimes called **baud**.

brightness Brightness is the intensity of light present in a color. See **HSB** for details.

bubble memory This is a form of memory storage that stores data (on a computer chip) in the form of non-volatile bubbles. Unlike conventional **RAM**, the information stored in these bubbles stays intact after power has been removed. Some computer printers, from companies like Canon, use bubble memory.

buffer This term refers to space that is typically reserved in memory to hold temporary file information. Information that is sent or *spooled* to a printer is usually placed in a buffer to await processing. This is especially true for large photographic files that are printed on **dye-sublimation** printers.

bundle Part of a software or hardware package, which may or may not be a good deal. When you purchase a product that's packaged with a product from another company at no additional cost, the extra product is considered to be "bundled" with the main product. In Louisiana, the natives would call the bundled product *lagniappe*–an extra or unexpected gift or benefit. I wouldn't buy a bundle just to get the software that the manufacturer has thrown in, but sometimes the combination can be irresistible. When I purchased Creative Lab's Sound Blaster 16/CD-ROM drive bundle, it came with several CD-ROM titles, including the now-obsolete Aldus PhotoStyler, *A Tour of the San Diego Zoo*, *Where in the World Is Carmen San Diego?* and *Grandma and Me*. From time to time, the software content of bundles will vary, so check the box before making a purchase. The *Grandma and Me* program, for instance, is no longer bundled, but the Discovery kit now includes more software and a microphone that was not included when I bought my kit at the beginning of the year. As always when contemplating any computer purchase–*caveat emptor*.

bus In the most strict, technical definition, a bus is a common pathway or channel on the computer's **motherboard** that connects multiple devices. It gets its name from real buses because a bus makes all of the stops on its route. This is true for digital buses too. All of the signals on the bus go to the different devices that are connected to it. A computer's internal bus is known as a *local bus* and connects the **CPU** (Central Processing Unit) chip to its memory and to controllers that attach to peripheral devices, such as **CD-ROM**, **hard drive**, and tape mechanisms. See **VL Bus** and **PCI Bus**.

bus slot For more information, see **expansion slot**. On your computer's **motherboard** you'll see rows of plastic and metal strips that look as if they're designed to have something inserted into them. They are. They are called **slots**, or *bus slots*, and accept printed circuit cards that allow accessories or devices to be attached to the motherboard.

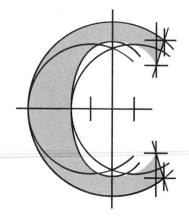

C Besides being the third letter of the alphabet, C is the name of a high-level programming language that's used to create the software you find on your computer dealer's shelves.

CAD Webster's defines a cad as a contemptible, ill-bred person, but the *Digital Imaging Dictionary* knows that it's an acronym for Computer-Aided Design. CAD is the use of computers to produce designs and drawings for engineering and scientific applications.

calibration A term used in Color Management Systems (**CMS**). Calibration stabilizes the inevitable variables in the way any device reproduces color. All kinds of variables—including your working environment—can affect the way a device is calibrated. To produce optimum results, all color-reproducing devices must maintain a consistent, calibrated state. A variety of calibration products are available depending on the device and manufacturer. For example, LightSource offers a monitor calibration tool called the Colortron for Macintosh systems that establishes a baseline to keep colors consistent throughout the reproduction process.

CCD A Charged Coupled Device is the same kind of light-gathering device used in flatbed **scanners**, digital cameras, and even video camcorders to convert the light passing through the lens into an electronic equivalent of the original image. These images become digitized by the CCD device. Most small-format digital cameras use a full-frame 24×36 mm CCD imager to deliver 36-bit color (12 bits per **RGB** color) digital images. The Sinar/Leaf CatchLight large-format back uses a 1.2×1.2-inch (3×3 cm) CCD chip to capture color images at 14 bits per pixel or 42-bit color. For pixel counters, this generates a image containing 4 million pixels at a resolution of 2048×2048 pixels.

Keep in mind that except for the Kodak **DCS** 460c Digital Camera, the CCD chips used in today's digital film backs for *large-format* cameras are colorblind. This is no big deal when making black-and-white images, but gets slightly more complicated when you have to make a color exposure. The only way to make a color exposure is to use filters that separate the image into its basic additive color components of red, green, and blue. For openers, this knocks your effective film speed down to an **exposure index** of 25–50, which may or may not be a problem for you depending on the subject matter being photographed. Filtration is typically accomplished through a front-end lens attachment, which can make using other lens attachments less than convenient. One way around the filtration problem is to use a shutter, which integrates the filter package into the electronic shutter. This leaves the front of the lens free to mount other devices, such as a compendium lens shade—which some large-format photographers feel is an indispensable accessory.

CCD linear array To understand how this form of medium- and large-format digital camera back works, we need to look at how scanners work, because these backs could more correctly be called "scanner backs."

Depending on their design, traditional flatbed scanners make one or three passes across an original lying on a flat piece of glass. Scanners use a CCD array consisting of several CCD elements arranged in a row on a single chip. Three-pass CCD scanners use a single linear array and rotate an **RGB** color wheel in front of the lens before each of the three passes are made. (Is this starting to sound familiar?) A single-pass scanner uses three linear arrays, which are respectively coated to filter red, blue, and green light. The same image data is focused onto each array simultaneously. Instead of a large CCD chip, scanner backs use a linear array of sensors that move across the 4×5 image area. Obviously this is not instantaneous, and scanning time will depend on whether a color or black-and-white image is being scanned.

It can take three to twelve minutes to scan some images, which makes the choice of subjects limited and the lighting requirements more critical, but does permit higher-resolution scans. The Dicomed Linear CCD Scan Back, for example, takes three and a half minutes to capture a full color image with its one-pass design. The Dicomed back has a traditional film holder shape and can create 36-bit (12 bits per color) images with a resolution of 6000×7520 pixels, with over eight stops of dynamic range. Like CCD designs, the Dicomed back doesn't cover the entire 4×5 frame. It is limited to 72×90 mm (2.8×3.5 inches) and the photographer can decide where to place that area within the 4×5 frame. The back's sensitivity is equivalent to conventional film having an ISO rating of 50/100/200 and is user-selectable. The CCD in Dicomed's' scanning back has an inherent equivalent to ISO 50, but through software that's included with the back, you can increase that sensitivity–to a certain extent–before the image data becomes noisy or unusable. Using a computer connected to the back, you can increase its ISO equivalent to a user's choice of either 100 or 200.

As is typical in large-format digital imaging, there is no free lunch. Scanning backs are typically larger than CCD backs, some even more so because they include optional hard disks to store large image data files. This makes them slightly heavier, and is one of the reasons Sinar Bron recommends a base plate support option that includes two rail clamps that provide additional support for the back. While the image area covered is larger than a CCD back, it is still slightly smaller than a full 4×5 area covered by a sheet film holder. A 150 mm or 180 mm lens would be considered "normal" for a scanning back. Because of the repeated shutter opening and closing that scanning backs require, you'll need to have an auto exposure shutter to maintain constant calibration.

CCH CorelCHART (graphics file format).

CD-MO Compact Disc-Magneto-Optical discs on which data can be written, erased, and rewritten.

CDR CorelDRAW! (graphics file format).

CD-ROM Compact Disc Read-Only Memory. This is a disc that resembles a musical CD-ROM but can contain all kinds of data–including photographs. The drives that use CD-ROM discs are called CD-ROM *drives*.

For trivia buffs only: Here's some background on where CD-ROM came from. When Sony and Phillips introduced the original CD audio specifications it was commonly called the **Red Book** standard, presumably because it was delivered in a red book. These specs, which provide for 2352 bytes of audio data and two layers of error detection, are the foundation on which all CD-based formats are based.

This was followed by the introduction of the initial CD-ROM standard, which is called the **Yellow Book**. Besides audio, this new standard allows for computer data (in Mode 1) and for compressed audio, video, and photographic data (in Mode 2). Discs that contain both modes are called *mixed mode*. The third iteration of this process extended Yellow Book specifications to include XA discs, which allow computer data to be coexist with compressed audio, video, and picture information. In effect, it combines the two modes found in the Yellow Book.

Next came the **Green Book** standard for CD-I (Compact Disc Interactive), which, like the XA mode, allows interleaving of computer data with compressed audio on the same track. One difference is that the CD-I track doesn't appear on the disc's table of contents, preventing audio CD players from playing CD-I tracks. Up to this point, all of the previous standards were designed for prerecorded discs.

The next step, the **Orange Book** standard, defined specifications for recordable CD-ROM discs. Part I of the Orange Book was written for **CD-MO** (Compact Disc-Magneto-Optical) discs, where data can be written erased, and rewritten. Part II defines standards for **CD-WO** (Compact Disc-Write-Once) where data cannot be erased. You'll often hear these later drives called **WORM** for *Write Once Read Many times*.

For the technically inclined: All these standards and specifications do not describe which file structure should be used when placing computer data onto a CD-ROM. That's why, several years ago, a group of industry representatives got together at Del Webb's High Sierra Hotel & Casino in Reno to draft a proposed CD-ROM file structure that could be read by both IBM-PCs and Macintoshes. Their original proposal was called the *High Sierra* format and several manufacturers issued discs using this format before it was officially adopted. As implemented by the International Standards Association, the new standard contained a few enhancements, and the resulting format was known as ISO 9660. Unfortunately, ISO 9660 and High Sierra are incompatible. Files on a CD-ROM disk in the ISO 9660 format can be read on IBM and compatible systems, Apple computers, and **UNIX** platforms.

Speaking of UNIX, the Rock Ridge Extensions to the ISO 9660 format enables the production of CD-ROMs which define a set of system use fields, allowing access to permission, file links, device nodes, UNIX file names and more. This format is not used extensively but *is* popular in the UNIX world.

Lastly, you should be aware that "hybrid" CDs are becoming a common form of distribution. These discs include multiple partitions, usually in Mac HFS (Hierarchical Filing System) and **DOS** formats. While this format makes it easier for software manufacturers, it can create minor problems for users. Fortunately there is third-party CD-ROM drive software that makes working with hybrids less stressful.

CD-ROM is about to undergo its biggest change since the format was introduced. Buoyed by the agreement on a standard for Digital Video Disk (**DVD**), industry leaders such as Phillips and Sony have agreed upon a new unified format for home video that promises to replace lower-quality VHS tapes with fully digital movies. Even before consumers other than the extremely well-heeled are watching *Batman Returns* on DVD, computer users will have access to these multiple-layer products that use a phase-change technology to pack even more information than the 650MB commonly found on CD-ROM. Called HDCD (High-Density Compact Disc) these discs will be able to store 2.6GB and 4.7GB of data. Two writable versions are planned: HDCD-E, an erasable high-density format that will allow users to write data to the disc, erase it, and re-write information on top of it. There will also be a WORM (Write Once Read Many times) version too. Both writable formats have an expected capacity of 2.6GB.

The development of the music CD drove the market for CD-ROM discs and drives. The introduction of DVD promises to have an even greater impact.

CD-WO Compact Disc-Write-Once are CD-ROM discs on which data cannot be erased.

CEPS Color Electronic Publishing Systems is a dedicated, computerized system used by printers for color management.

CFR Color Film Recorder. A device that translates images onto photographic film. All desktop film recorders work in essentially the same way: A camera is enclosed in a small box and is focused on a very high-resolution black-and-white monitor. It makes three exposures of the image, each through separate red, blue, and green filters to produce the final image. If this sounds slow to you—it can be.

CGM Computer Graphics **Metafile**. A **vector** graphics format that is designed to be portable from one PC-based program to another.

characterization A Color Management System (CMS) term that establishes the relationship of your calibrated device to what is referred to as a *device-independent reference color space* or RCS. This "color space," which you can think of as the Mr. Roger's Neighborhood where all color devices get along, describes how a device reads, displays, and stores color values. **Photo CD** devices, for example, store color in a format Kodak calls **YCC**. This converts data that was originally **RGB** into one part of what scientists call luminance but the rest of us call brightness (this is the Y component) and two parts (the CC) of chrominance, or color plus hue. This system keeps file size under control while maintaining the Photo CD's "photographic" look. Monitors display color in the RGB color space. In the device-independent reference color space, both Photo CD and the monitor share a common basis in color.

chip A piece of silicon or similar material on top of which an **integrated circuit**, or hundreds or thousands of circuits are built. The internal design and circuits of a microprocessor chip is referred to as the chip's *architecture*. The chips used by a microcomputer handles all of the information that goes in (**input**) or out (**output**) of it.

circuit board A flat plastic strip upon which electronic circuits are printed, which is why they are often called *printed circuit boards*.

CISC Complex Instruction Set Computing. Until recently, this microprocessor chip design was the most common type. It is gradually being replaced with a faster, less-expensive **RISC** chip.

clock speed The clock circuit of a computer uses vibrations that are generated by a quartz crystal, not unlike the one in your quartz wrist watch, to generate a stream of pulses to the **CPU**. You'll be able to spot the clock on the **motherboard**, because it looks like a tiny sardine can. How fast the CPU of a microcomputer operates is measured by its clock speed, which is measured in MegaHertz (MHz), or thousands of cycles per second. The faster the clock speed, the faster the CPU can process data. Therefore if you see a computer labeled 486/50, you know it has a 486 CPU running at a clock speed of 50 MHz.

clone (1) Sometimes you will hear IBM-compatible computers called "clones," although that term has taken on a pejorative connotation since former clone makers like Compaq Computer and Dell actually sell more IBM-compatible personal computers than IBM does.

Now there are Mac-compatibles that everyone is calling "clones." Radius offers Video Vision Workstation, a Macintosh-based video-editing system, and Power Computing has announced that the company will start shipping computers using the Macintosh operating system. Both companies will build Mac clones, although they can't label them "Macintosh." Power Computing started shipping Mac-compatibles at prices $600 less than similar Power Macintosh computers. Power Computing clones will include quadruple-speed **CD-ROM** drives, compared to the double-speed CD-ROM drives typically found in Apple Macintoshes.

Although Apple includes software bundles with their Performa models, software bundles for the "standard" models are quite rare. On the other hand, Power Computing will bundle ClarisWorks 3.0, Quicken 5.0, Now Up-To-Date 3.0, Now Utilities, and Now Contact 3.0. The Power Computing models also include FWB Inc.'s Hard Disk Toolkit and CD-ROM Toolkit, 300 Bitstream Type 1 and **TrueType** fonts, and America Online.

Whew! Should you buy a Mac clone instead of the real thing? Here are a few points to keep in mind: Mac-compatibles have been licensed by Apple, and because of that, there should be few of the compatibility problems that plagued early IBM-compatible machines. Prices should be competitive with "real" Macs, but I expect Apple retailers, especially the computer superstores, to aggressively price Apple-labeled equipment. This brings the choice between Apple Macintosh models and clones down to performance, bundled software and hardware, and most importantly, price.

(2) *Clone* is also a tool or command found in many image enhancement programs. In Adobe Photoshop, the rubber stamp tool is used to clone or choose part of an image and recreate that selection in the same or another part of the image. For example: I scanned a black-and-white graphic of a rabbit to use in a flyer, but this bunny was holding a magnifying glass I wanted to remove. I used Adobe Photoshop's eraser tool to remove the magnifying glass, but this left gaps in the bunny's paw. So I used the rubber stamp to clone part of the bunny's fur and rubber-stamped the missing fur onto the paw. I used the pencil tool to touch it up and when I was finished the bunny looked like he never held anything.

CMOS (1) A Complimentary Metal Oxide Semiconductor is a type of Large-Scale Integrated (LSI) circuit that has low power requirements, is generally available, and has modest performance capabilities.

(2) This is also what PC users typically call the chip where the system defaults are stored along with any changes to system parameters. Since it is RAM and is volatile, the CMOS chip is battery-powered to keep the information "hot." CMOS is similar to **PRAM** for the Macintosh.

CMS Color Management Systems (CMS) software helps you produce accurate reproduction of your original color images. A good CMS must address two major aspects—**calibration** and **characterization**—and all successful systems must include both of them. Color management systems are (mostly) software-based systems used to match the color you see on your monitor to the color from the output device—printer or film recorder—so that what you see on the screen is what you get as output. You might think of this as the last step in the WYSIWYG process. Recently, programs like Adobe's Photoshop and PageMaker began including Kodak's Precision Color Management Software as part of their package. The software alone is useless unless you have *device profiles* (an integral part of any color management system) for the monitors and output devices that you use. Device profiles are small software utilities that match the characteristics of various input and output equipment and must be created for specific monitors, such as the NEC XE15, and output devices, like a Mirus film recorder. Some companies, like Fargo Electronics, provide their own CMS for their printers.

The reason the "mostly" appears at the beginning of the definition is that some color management systems include devices that attach to your monitor to allow precise matching of a special color, such as Kodak Yellow or Petty Blue.

CMX Corel Presentation Exchange (graphics file format).

CMYK Cyan, Magenta, Yellow, and Black. Yeah, I know black doesn't begin with a "K," but it does end with one. Blame this tortured acronym on the same printing industry that has saddled us with "picas."

The primary additive colors of red, blue, and green, when added together, produce white light. In the areas that they overlap, red and blue form magenta, green and red produce yellow, and green and blue create cyan. These resulting colors are *subtractive*, and filters using varying intensities of the colors are used when making Type C prints from color negatives. When the subtractive colors are added together they form, not black, but a dark brown. That's why black must be added, and why the four-color process uses cyan, magenta, yellow, and black for accurate photographic reproduction.

Darkroom workers who make prints from color negatives don't have to bother with "K" or black filters to produce prints. For magazine repro-duction, however, an image must be separated into varying percentages of cyan, magenta, yellow, and black, which is why CMYK film output are called *separations*. Most comprehensive digital imaging programs can produce color separations directly from within the program, eliminating another generation and increasing quality during the reproduction process. Computer printers also use CMYK dyes and inks to produce accurate, photographic quality prints.

color depth resolution Measures the amount of color information each pixel can display. *See* **bit resolution**.

color matching method (CMM) A routine used by a color manage-ment system to apply transformations to color data.

color temperature Unlike the eye, which has a brain attached to it, cameras are literal recorders of the color they see. That's because the balance of colors found in different kinds of natural and artificial light is measured as *color temperature* using the Kelvin scale as a system of measurement. All light sources have different colors, and while the human brain makes corrections for a white shirt viewed outdoors or inside under incandescent light, the camera cannot. (Daylight, for instance, has a color temperature of 5,500 degrees Kelvin, while typical incandescent lights run around 3,000 degrees.) The higher the color temperature, the cooler (bluer) the color is. Conversely, the lower the number, the warmer (redder) it is. To compensate for this difference, film manufacturers develop film balanced for specific lighting conditions. Filters can be used, both on the light source and the camera lens to balance the color to *neutral*–a number around 5,500 degrees Kelvin. Color temperature is important in digital imaging, too, because it is necessary to balance the colors seen on a computer monitor to that of the output device. *See* **color management systems**.

COMDEX Acronym for Communications and Data Exposition, the largest computer trade show in the world, held just before Thanksgiving in Las Vegas. A slightly smaller show is held in the spring at various locations, including Atlanta, Georgia. Fall COMDEX is crowded, noisy, and overflowing with the sights and sounds of contemporary computing. For five days in November, over 200,000 computer users jam the show halls searching for their own, personal, digital holy grail. Although COMDEX has its share of silly products, like a talking mouse and a leather shoulder holster for Apple's Newton personal data assistant, there are plenty of more practical software and hardware offerings for anyone interested in multimedia or digital imaging.

COMDEX is now owned by a Japanese company called Softbank. The fall 1996 show was the first under the new ownership, and it was both bigger and better than any previous show. The future looks bright for COMDEX.

compatible The ability to operate correctly with another, different brand or type of computer. The most common type of compatible computer, at least until recently, was the IBM-compatible machine. In the early days of the IBM-PC standard, few computers (Compaq was a notable exception) were 100 percent compatible, and peripherals that were compatible with one machine may did not necessarily work with another. Currently, this is a non-issue.

Now we have Mac-compatibles too, but few problems have surfaced since early Mac-compatible manufacturers used genuine Apple components to minimize compatibility problems.

composite monitor A color video monitor than accepts *composite video* information composed of video data and synchronizing signals.

compression This is a technique that lets you make a file smaller, and consequently take up less space, by removing irrelevant information from the file. Compression programs make files smaller by reducing the amount of unneeded space it occupies on a disk. As the resolution of a photographic image increases, so does its file size. As file size increases greater demands are made on your hard disk and CPU. That's why compression technology was invented. Compression is a method of removing unneeded data to make a file smaller without losing any data, or in the case of a photographic file, image quality.

Having a smaller file while retaining image quality means your hardware can work on the files faster and you can store more images on your hard disk. There are many techniques and technologies for compressing graphics and how well each works depends on what is more important to you: file size or image quality.

Some digitizing processes, like Kodak's Photo CD, depend on compression techniques to work. During the digitizing process, each image is prescanned and displayed on the Photo CD's workstation monitor. The operator checks the orientation of the image to see if it is portrait (vertical) or landscape (horizontal), and begins the final, high-resolution scan. Each digital image is sent to the workstation for color and density correction, and data compression techniques are used to reduce each image's original 18-megabyte size to 4.5 megabytes. These compressed files are written onto the CD by the discwriter, and the thermal printer creates an index print that's placed in the front of the CD's jewel case.

PKZIP is a popular compression shareware program for IBM-PC and compatible machines, and similar programs, like StuffIt, are available for the Macintosh. Remember, a decompression utility is needed to bring the file back to its original size.

No compression program can compress a 18MB photograph to fit on a single disk, but spreading it across several **floppy disks** will let you handle larger image files. Compression may be the least expensive way to transport images but it has two potential drawbacks. The **service bureau** must have the identical software (and same version number) you used to compress the file. If you send six disks and request a ten-dollar 35 mm slide, your lab may charge a premium for extra handling. Depending on how often you do this, compression software may not be the least expensive way to get your images to a service bureau.

CompuServe A computer network that can be accessed by subscribers to the service by using a **modem**. One of the best ways to stay on top of digital imaging techniques and technical breakthroughs is by reading magazines, like *PHOTO>Electronic Imaging*, that devote pages to the subject. Publications like Rohn Engh's *PhotoStockNotes* help keep you abreast of trends on the business side of digital and stock images. The problem with most print media is that there is usually a two-to-three month lead time between when an article is written and when it's published. Books, including this one, suffer from the same fate. Using an on-line service lets you get up-to-date information as well as minor software upgrades (especially drivers for printers, scanners, and monitors) from the companies that produce these products.

CompuServe sells starter kits that include software called CompuServe Information Manager (CIM) which is available for Windows and for Macintosh computers. CompuServe has a minimum monthly billing (less than $10) that includes a number of hours of access time. Time that exceeds that amount is billed additionally. Think of it like cable TV. The basic monthly rates include basic service, but if you want any premium services, like the Photography Forum on CIS, it will cost a little extra. But the Kodak Photo CD Forum is included in the basic service. You can run up a big monthly bill like a cable TV junkie, but since CompuServe has lower rates after normal working hours, there are ways to keep your billing quite modest. Access in most metropolitan areas is through a local phone number, so you won't have any toll charges to deal with, except in certain areas.

One of the fun places CIM can take you is the Photography Forum. CompuServe calls sections of the network where people with common interests congregate forums. There are forums for everything, including model railroads, where I also check in from time to time. A forum's message section allows you to post messages on what amounts to a community bulletin board, eliciting feedback and comments from photographers all over the world. If you want to keep it private, use **e-mail**. The libraries are places where members of the forum post images and **shareware** and or **freeware**.

When data is sent to an on-line service it is *uploaded*. When data is retrieved from CIS, it is *downloaded*. As you can see, the Photography Forum can be a good source of shareware and freeware specifically designed for photographers. You can also go to the on-line libraries listed to download information from the different conferences mentioned in the Newsflash. From time to time, conferences are held with experts available to answer your questions. These are live conferences and can include hundreds of participants all over the world, electronically connected. Some may ask questions and offer opinions, while others (called "lurkers") sit quietly and absorb what's being said. The first time you participate in a worldwide conference you will know what Buckminster Fuller meant by "global village."

Another forum—for pros only—is called the Photo Pro Forum and it has sixteen sections, including some reserved for members of the Professional Photographers of America (PPA) and the American Society of Media Photographers (ASMP), covering everything from darkroom techniques to cameras to stock photography and business matters. There's even a "Photography NOT!" section for off-topic discussions.

There's more to CompuServe than both the Kodak Photo CD and these two photography forums. Fuji Photo Film and Polaroid have forums and there are tons of forums on Microsoft Windows and Macintosh-related subjects. Large software manufacturers, like Claris and Adobe, have their own forums where you can download "updaters" that can fix any of your program's bugs with or just ask questions of experts about a given program. Smaller manufacturers, like Berkeley Systems, can be found in one of the Vendors forums that gather ten or so companies together. It would be hard not to find answers to your business or photographic questions.

There are fun parts of CompuServe too. Film critic Roger Ebert has his own forum and you can download or read reviews of recent movies. I was able to read a review of *Jurassic Park* (he hated it; a big thumbs-down) before it opened in my town. And *Consumer Reports* has a forum where I recently checked information on tires for my Jeep.

As of this writing CompuServe has 4.5 million subscribers, while rival America Online has 5 million. CIS's parent company, H & R Block, has even talked about spinning CompuServe off as a separate company, but so far that has not happened. In the late 1990s, all on-line services face the same threat: competition from the Internet and World Wide Web.

configuration Nikon was, perhaps, the first camera manufacturer to use the word *system* in describing the various lenses, bodies, and accessories they offered. What was unusual at that time was the way that all these optical and mechanical components worked together to form a photographic system. Like a good camera system, a computer is made up of several elements, both hardware and software. Together, these elements will make up your computer system. What size and type of components are used in the system define a computer's *configuration*. For example, the configuration for my Power Macintosh system is 24MB RAM, 500MB hard disk, double-speed CD-ROM drive, 100MB Iomega ZIP **removable media** drive, Nikon Coolscan scanner, and Epson Stylus color printer. A configuration, therefore, describes the components and capabilities of your computer system.

control key Usually abbreviated CTRL, used with other keys to perform a specific operation within a PC program. CTRL-P, for instance is often used as the print command. While Macintosh computers have a CTRL key, more often than not the command key (it looks like a four-leaf clover lying its side) is used for command-key applications. Command-P is the standard Macintosh print command in all programs.

control panel (1) In the Macintosh system, a Control Panel is a small program that does something specific for your computer system or application. Each utility has its own panel for controlling various features or settings. Back when Apple Computer's System 6 was the only game in town, they were called CDEVs.

(2) In Microsoft Windows, the Control Panel window contains many small utilities that allow you to customize the way your interface looks as well as adjusting the settings of hardware and software.

Convolver An Adobe Photoshop-compatible **plug-in** from MetaTools (formerly HSC software). Convolver combines many different Adobe Photoshop filters and commands, such as brightness, contrast, sharpness, and others, into a single tool that can apply two different effects to an image at the same time. This speeds up the image enhancement process and adds some functionality missing in the original filter. Sharpen, for example, can only be applied one way. Convolver allows sharpening to occur as specific percentages of sharpening.

You'll notice that Convolver is a different kind of plug-in as soon as you launch it. Its diamond-shaped 3-D interface contains two windows: a small "Before" and larger "Preview." In the upper left-hand corner are buttons that activate one of Convolver's three modes: Explore, Design, and Tweak. When one of the modes is selected, controls that affect the others are dimmed or "asleep." When the Explore mode is selected, three more buttons appear, allowing users try different filters the results of which are displayed in fifteen variations or *tiles* in the Preview window. Clicking the Mutate Genes button generates fifteen new tiles. You can click on any one of the fifteen and this tile becomes the basis for which the next round of mutations is built. Two other buttons control how much each tile is different from one another. The Genetic Diversity button has a pop-up menu that lets you set five different levels of diversity from Minimum to Maximum. Gene Influences lets you vary your choice of: Blur/Sharpen, Embossing, Edge Detection, Hue, Saturation, Brightness, Contrast, and Tint. You can select any or all of them to be used in the mutations. Design Mode lets you apply two different filters at one time and contains sliding arrows that allow you to set how much or little the effects will be implemented. Results are displayed as tiles in the Preview window. Tweak Mode contains fourteen filter controls that allow you to tweak the image's color, sharpness, and contrast.

MetaTools's manual recommends you start in Explore mode, add effects in Design mode and touch up the finished image in Tweak mode. In practice, I was more comfortable doing the opposite. I start in Tweak mode by using the Sharpen control, because all Photo CDs and many scanned images invariably need some sharpening. As described before, Convolver displays a percentage in the bottom of the windows indicating how much sharpening is being applied. Most of the percentages I used were smaller than the large numbers (usually over 100 percent) required for Adobe Photoshop's Unsharp Mask. Then I use the Fade to Gray setting to make the color as neutral as possible and kick the Contrast up a bit before moving into Design mode. Convolver's Tweak mode contains controls that are available within Adobe Photoshop, and, for the first time, enables you to quantify the changes you make. Using Design and Explore modes lets you produce effects not possible with any other Adobe Photoshop add-on.

coprocessor An additional microprocessor chip that assists your computer's CPU functions and helps speed up mathematical calculations used by spreadsheet programs and other math-intensive applications.

copy protection To encode the information in a computer program in such a way as to make unauthorized copying impossible. At one time, copy protection was quite popular with many programs, but now seems to be used mainly for games and entertainment software. The Software Publishers Association (SPA) calls this illegal copying "piracy," but you and I know it by another word: *theft*.

The basic rule of software ownership is that you should own one copy of a program for each machine it runs on. If you use Claris's FileMaker Pro for your clients' database, you must own one copy of that program for each computer on which it is installed. The only exception I know of is that some, but not all, software licenses specify you can have a copy of the program installed on your office machine *and* a laptop—if you only use one of them at a time. For companies and studios with a small number of computers, owning multiple copies of a program shouldn't be too much of a financial strain, especially if you purchase the software from mail order discounters. If you have more than five computers, you may be able to save money by looking into "site licenses." Most software companies offer site licenses which allow you to install multiple copies of their programs for less than the "per each" cost of the software multiplied by the number of computers in your business. These licenses must be negotiated with each individual company, and the company often makes good deals on subsequent upgrades too.

CP/M Control Program for Microprocessors. A once-popular but now defunct operating system for the 8080 and Z80 microprocessors developed by Gary Kildall of Digital Research. CP/M had its heyday in the early 1980s. Computer folklore (perhaps apocryphal) has it that in the early days, when IBM was searching for an operating system, they approached Digital Research to license CP/M for their about-to-be-launched PC, but Gary Kildall was hang-gliding and couldn't take their meeting. Bill Gates of Microsoft was, however, able to take the call and the rest is, as they say, history.

CPU Central Processing Unit. The choice of which platform to use boils down to the microchip or *CPU*, Central Processing Unit, that powers the computer. All cameras use the same kind of photo/optical engineering, and you can make great photographs with an old Nikon F or a brand-new N90s. But digital imagers need to have enough computing power to handle the kind of images they will be working with. Shooting wildlife or sports photography is possible with a 50 mm lens, but the photographic experience will be much better—and less frustrating—when armed with a 400 or 800 mm lens. Choosing the right computer is first a matter of finding one with enough power to process digital images, to minimize frustration, and to expedite creativity by processing that data as fast as possible.

There are two basic families of CPUs: Intel and Motorola. Intel and similar chips are used in IBM-compatible PCs, while Motorola makes the chips for Macintosh and compatible machines. For the PC platforms, there are alternatives to the Intel microprocessor chips but they all follow Intel's standard. How well any chip processes data is determined by how many bits of information it can process at one time. The larger the number of **bits** a chip can process simultaneously, the faster it can process. Think of it as a highway. The more lanes you provide, the more cars can travel on it at one time. A 32-bit CPU, for example, processes data twice as fast as a 16-bit model.

To help identify the different classes, computer chips have numbers or (lately) names to identify them. When someone refers to a "386," it's usually an Intel 80386 32-bit computer chip. Intel followed the 386 chip with a 486 and later a 586, which they named **Pentium**, both of which are significantly faster than the 386 chip. Apple Computer's chips are made by Motorola and their 32-bit equivalent to the 386 chip is called 68030 or just "030." Apple's faster chips are the 040 and PowerPC, which competes for raw processing power with Intel's Pentium.

Besides the number of bits it can process at one time, the most important aspect of the CPU is how fast it does it. If the path defines the number of lanes on the highways, the clock speed defines how fast the cars can travel on those lanes. This is measured by the CPU's **clock speed**. Until recently, Apple has hidden the clock speed of its computers. If you see a Power Mac 8100/100, you know that the last number refers to clock speed, but you'll need an Apple catalog to know that the 8100 designation is used for their top-of-the-line computer using the PowerPC chip developed jointly with IBM and Motorola.

Processing speed is extremely important to digital photographers. It's like shooting photographs under low light conditions. Under these difficult lighting situations, you'll usually switch to films with a faster ISO speed so you can capture images more easily. The speed of the CPU is equally important when manipulating digital images because of the large number of bits that make up a digital image. While slower microprocessors can work, as the traffic reporters say: expect delays. These processing delays can vary from annoying to maddening depending on what you are doing with the image. No matter which kind of computer you decide to use, you should get one with the fastest CPU you can afford. If you prefer an IBM-PC or compatible, you should only consider a computer with a 486 or Pentium processor. Macintosh users should stick with models containing 68040 or Power PC chips.

crash If you don't know what a computer crash is, eventually you're going to find out. The read/write heads on a hard disk float a microscopic distance above a hard disk's platter. Misalignment, dust, and grime can cause that head to "crash" into the disk's surface. When that happens, it is possible that all or some of your data will be lost.

cross-platform The ability to work on Macintosh or PC-based computers. A program or file (like Kodak's Photo CD disc and file format) is said to be *cross-platform* when a version is available for both systems, or when the same file format can be read by both platforms.

CRT Cathode-Ray Tube. A propeller-head's word for the TV-like picture tube inside your monitor.

cryptography This is not a new form of photography, but is the art and science of transforming data into an **encrypted** form so that it may not be read by unauthorized persons, those who do not have the password or key.

cybernetics The comparative study of computers and the human nervous system. Over the years the prefix *cyber* has been added to many terms in a questionably hip attempt to create even more buzzwords. If the urge comes over you to add "cyber" to some other word (Does "cyberlunch" bother you as much as it does me?), resist it.

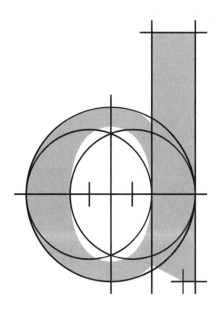

data Electrical signals processed by a computer to create information or images, such as photographs.

database An organized collection of related data in the form of files that can be built, maintained, and printed with a computer. Database programs that hold photographs, graphics, sounds, and video clips have been dubbed multimedia databases or **imagebase** programs.

DCS Digital Camera System. A term used by Eastman Kodak to describe a system of digital camera. If this class of cameras resembles conventional 35 mm professional cameras it's because, with just a few exceptions, they are based on existing silver-based designs.

Kodak's professional digital cameras represent a strategic alliance with 35 mm camera manufacturers like Nikon and Canon. Their family of digital cameras are essentially digital imaging backs attached to Nikon and

Canon camera bodies. Since many of the cameras are similar, let's look at what they have in common.

All the cameras use a full-frame **CCD** imager to deliver 36-bit color (12 bits per RGB color), the ability to store images on **PCMCIA** cards, and a built-in microphone for voice annotation. Once users are ready to retrieve their images, the cameras also serve as card readers. A standard **SCSI** cable connects the camera directly to a Macintosh or PC computer. Software shipped with the camera enables Macintosh users to transfer image information from the camera's card reader directly to Adobe Photoshop, and separate software allows PC users to move image information into **TWAIN**-compliant applications.

The Kodak DCS 420 digital camera features a full-frame CCD imager delivering a resolution of 1.5 million pixels, at a burst rate of five images in 2.25 seconds. The DCS 420 consists of a special electronic back fixed to the body of a Nikon N90 camera. Its battery pack is good for one thousand images per charge. Users can select equivalent **ISO** film speeds from 50 to 400 in color and from 100 to 800 in black and white. The Kodak professional DCS 460 digital camera features a 3,060 x 2,036 pixel CCD imager delivering a resolution of 6 million pixels. The imager resides in an electronic back that is attached to a Nikon N90 body camera. Once the camera is powered up, the time it takes to make the first shot is only 0.25 second. Subsequent images can be captured every twelve seconds. The DCS 460 features a battery pack good for at least three hundred images per charge, with a recharge time of one hour. Both the DCS 420 and 460 support virtually all of the standard Nikon N90 functions, including autofocus, self-timing, and a range of metering modes. They accept all Nikon F-mount lenses offered for the film version of the camera. The DCS 460 camera is available in three models: DCS 460c (color), DCS 460m (black and white), and DCS 460ir (infrared; available only by special order).

All models ship with the camera, an AC adapter/charger, Macintosh cables and driver software, and manuals. Professionals using medium-format cameras will be able to capture high-resolution digital images with Kodak's digital back for several 120 and 4 × 5 models that accept interchangeable backs. The Kodak Professional DCS 465 digital camera back features an image resolution of 3,060 × 2,036 pixels, single-shot color exposure, and 36-bit color with a sensitivity equivalent to an ISO film speed of 100. You've probably already figured out that the sensor is based on the same technology now being used in Kodak's DCS 400-series digital cameras. Kodak is working with camera manufacturers, such as Hasselblad and Sinar, to adapt the DCS 465 to their equipment.

In 1995, Kodak announced the EOS DCS 5, a new high-performance, megapixel digital camera based on Canon's EOS-1N camera. Developed in cooperation with Canon, the EOS DCS 5 camera shares many characteristics with the Kodak DCS 420 camera, including a burst rate of 2.3 images per second for ten images. The camera features all the advanced camera functions of the Canon EOS-1N: a 1.5 megapixel CCD sensor (1,524 × 1,012 pixels), 36-bit color, removable **PCMCIA** storage (both hard disk and flash memory cards), a battery pack capable of delivering up to one thousand images per charge, and a built-in microphone for voice annotation. The camera provides exposure equivalents from ISO 100 to 400 in color and 200 to 800 in black and white. A SCSI cable connects the camera to the computer and software lets Macintosh and PC users acquire image information from the camera's card reader. Kodak and Canon are also planning to produce two other digital cameras. Canon will market the EOS DCS 3 digital camera, which captures 1.3 million pixels at equivalent film speeds up to ISO 1600. In addition, a 6-million-pixel EOS DCS camera is schedule to be marketed by both companies.

default An automatic decision that your software or hardware makes for you, which will automatically be carried out unless you intervene and change the settings. Most programs allow the default setting to be changed simply by typing in your own preferences.

device resolution Refers to the number of dots per inch (dpi) that any given device, such as a monitor or printer, can produce. Device resolution for computer monitors varies from 60 to 120 dpi. Don't confuse this with screen resolution, which only refers to the number of dots per inch in the **line screen** used by printers to reproduce a photograph. Screen resolution is measured in lines per inch (lpi). Image resolution refers to the amount of information stored in a photograph and is typically expressed in pixels per inch (ppi.) The image resolution of a photograph determines how big the file is. The important thing to remember is that the higher the image resolution, the more disk space it takes and the longer it will take to print or image.

dialog box This is a window that occasionally appears in many programs to allow users to communicate with the software in order to achieve a specific result. The most basic example of a dialog box is the one that appears when you give the print command. By entering data in this window you can instruct the printer how many copies to print, in that order, and whether you want the image printed in color or black and white—assuming you have a color printer. Dialog boxes, or *dialogs* for short, are extremely important when working with filter plug-ins within image-manipulation programs, like Adobe Photoshop. In this case, the dialog lets you specify how an image will be enhanced and gives digital photographers control over how the final image will appear.

digital This is information represented by numbers, or in Max Head-room's case "a person translated as data." Computers use information measured in bits or *binary digits*. **Binary** is a mathematical system based on the numbers one and zero, and electrical signals represented by positive and negative (1 = current on, 0 = current off) electrical current. Each electronic signal becomes one bit, and to represent more complex numbers or images, computers combine these signals into larger, 8-bit groups called **bytes**.

digital camera A camera that uses **CCD** (Charged Coupled Device) technology to convert images into **pixels**. A charged coupled device is the same kind of light-gathering device used in video camcorders to convert the light passing through the lens into an electronic equivalent of the original image. These images then become digitized by the CCD. Most small-format digital cameras, those having a shape and design similar to conventional 35 mm cameras, use a full-frame 24×36 mm CCD imager to deliver 36-bit color (12 bits per RGB color) digital images.

The current generation of digital still cameras fall into three general categories: digital point-and-shoot, 35 mm-style field cameras, and professional studio equipment. The old adage of "you get what you pay for" strictly applies here. The first group contains the equivalent of those popular, auto-everything, point-and-shoot 35 mm cameras, and are designed to be used by non-professionals to capture images used in applications where ease of capture and low cost are more important than image quality. Point-and-shooters tend to be people such as real estate agents, insurance adjusters, and other documentarians who want to paste

Looking as much like a pair of binoculars as a digital point-and-shoot camera, Kodak's DC40 produces image quality equal to a base level Photo CD scan, making it ideal for use in non-professional image making.

their photographs into desktop published documents that will be printed on 300 dpi laser or inkjet printers. Digital point-and-shoot cameras are also great for having fun. If you want to take a picture of the new baby or boat and paste it into a letter to grandma, these cameras will do a great job. Expect to pay for the convenience, however. Most cameras in this category are pushing the $1,000 mark, and the higher the resolution, the higher the price.

If you want to move up to a pro-quality camera with interchangeable lenses, the next step is a digital field camera, most of which are based on conventional 35 mm camera bodies. This is a big step, because prices jump from under $1,000 to over $10,000. These cameras are used by photo-journalists on tight deadlines and photographers who must do their work on-location. They use the same lenses as most pros already use, so they can be instantly integrated into a camera system. Resolution of this class varies from modest to high, and their current price limits their use to professional photojournalists, or the well-heeled. The high-end digital cameras and camera backs are strictly aimed at professional in-studio use.

These cameras are designed to be used by advertising photographers who create images from art directors' sketches and often convert finished images directly into separations suitable for printing in four-color publications.

Some digital camera backs require bulky view cameras and must be directly connected to a computer. Some also require special high output lighting to minimize image capture time. These cameras and camera backs create megapixel images in large file sizes but capture the high quality needed for advertising and catalog work. The Sinar/Leaf CatchLight large-format back uses a 1.2 × 1.2-inch (3 × 3 cm) CCD chip to capture color images at 14 bits per pixel, or 42-bit color. For all of you pixel counters out there this generates a image containing four million pixels at a resolution of 2,048 × 2,048 pixels. This single-exposure back provides a light sensitivity equivalent to ISO 100 film (you can set your light meter at 100) and produces an image having a dynamic range in excess of nine stops. The Sinar/Leaf DCB II back uses a similar design, but is capable of up to three exposures in color or black and white and features a sensitivity equivalent of ISO 200 in black and white, ISO 25 in color. The Dicomed BigShot back uses a larger 6 × 6 cm CCD that can capture an image with a resolution of 4,096 × 4,096 pixels.

One of the most unusual digital cameras is Connectix's QuickCam. This golf ball–shaped (and sized) device is both a video and still digital camera. Image resolution is 320 × 240 pixels in 4-bit grayscale, and video images are captured at fifteen frames per second (at 160 × 120 resolution), instead of the video standard of 30 fps, but it only costs $99. The camera has a 65-degree field of view providing the equivalent of a 38 mm lens on a 35 mm camera, and focus is fixed from 18 inches to infinity. The software that's included lets you capture a single-frame image in either **BMP** or **TIFF** formats. The QuickCam even has a built-in microphone to capture audio. The Macintosh version connects to the computer's serial port, and a parallel port version is available for Windows.

digitize To put into digital form; e.g., a **scanner** can be used to digitize photographs.

DIMM The newest computers have switched from **SIMM** (Single In-line Memory Module) to Dual In-line Memory Module, that have RAM chips mounted on both sides of the circuit board. This means the motherboard can hold more memory using the same number of RAM slots. But, as is typical in most computer hardware innovations, SIMMs will not fit a DIMM slot, and vice versa. Several companies have, however, introduced DIMM converters that allow to SIMMs to be installed in an adapter that will fit a DIMM slot. This allows users to save their old SIMMs when upgrading to a DIMM-based computer.

disc When an image or file is recorded onto an optical disc, a laser beam cuts or melts small indentations into its surface. To playback, a typical drive uses a similar laser to read those dents and translates them into data—or photographs. This means that round, flat objects made with this laser technology are properly called *discs*. Magnetic media drives, on the other hand, use the same kind of technology that's been used on floppy disks since they were introduced. A disk is coated with magnetic material, and a read/write head records the files or images onto the disk. On playback, the same kind of head reads the magnetically encoded data and displays the files on your monitor. These round objects are properly called *disks*. Sometimes you'll see **Photo CD** discs erroneously referred to as "disks," but in this book I'll use the correct terminology: Hard disks and similar storage media will be called "disks" while CD-ROM, magneto-optical, and Photo CD discs will always be called "discs."

disk *See* **floppy disk** and **hard disk**.

disk crash The failure of a disk, usually caused by the read/write head (of any drive) coming in touch (crashing) with the disk surface. (*See* **crash**.) This can never happen to drives, like some manufactured by Iomega, that use the **Bernoulli box** principle.

diskette The original floppy disks were 8 inches in size and flopped around quite a bit. The next generation measured 5¼ inches, and like the originals were comprised of a thin, flexible magnetic disk housed inside a paper covering. Since they were smaller than the original disk, they were immediately called *diskettes*. When the plastic-shelled 3½-inch disks were introduced the were called *micro floppy disks*. Few computer users use the term *diskette* anymore. For more details, see **floppy disk**.

display *See* **monitor**.

distributed processing A technique that reduces the load on the **CPU** by transferring part of the processing function to other processors either inside the computer or to other computers in a multi-computer or multi-user system.

dithering A graphics display or printing process that uses a combination of dots or textures to create the impression of a continuous-tone grayscale or color image.

DMA An acronym for Direct Memory Access. Expansion cards installed in a PC use it to access system memory directly without going through the CPU.

document (1) Information about a specific subject in computer-readable form. A business letter and an Adobe PageMaker file containing text and photographs are both considered documents. To some, *document* is synonymous with file.

(2) What you see on the screen is a document as differentiated from a file, which is considered the location in which that information is stored on a hard or floppy disk.

documentation The manuals, user's guide, and tutorials that are packed with the shrink-wrapped software that you just purchased. The purpose of the documentation is to tell (or teach) you how to use the software. For small applications like Alien Skin's Black Box plug-ins, documentation may consist of a 28-page booklet, but the documentation for the latest version of Adobe Photoshop includes a User's Guide, Quick Reference Card, Getting Started manual, Tutorial, and a 28-page booklet entitled "Beyond the Basics."

DOS Disc Operating System. Often the Microsoft Disk Operating System (**MS-DOS**) is referred to as simply DOS.

dot gain An increase in the size of the dots of a halftone image during the printing process. This is inherent in the printing process and the best way to avoid having your images degraded during printing is to plan ahead, anticipating the effect of increased dot size.

dot-matrix A type of printer (not often seen anymore) that uses a print head to strike a ribbon, much like a typewriter. Unlike a typewriter there are no discreet letters. A dot-matrix printer forms text (or graphics) by having a print head that uses tiny pins (often just nine of them) to form every letter of the alphabet. These printers use a dot hammer to strike the pins. Depending on the printer, some use one or two hammers. Consequently, with all that hammerin' going on, dot-matrix printers can be slow and noisy, but their ability to use multi-part continuous paper to print several carbonless copies at a time make them popular in the retail environment, like your neighborhood video store. In the Mac world, the classic dot-matrix printer is the ImageWriter, while Epson set the standard for many years for PCs.

dot pitch The classic definition of dot pitch is the distance between the red (center) dot of two adjoining pixel triads on a monitor. The smaller this number, the sharper the picture will be. A good monitor, like the NEC MultiSync XE17 has a dot pitch of .28 mm. Anything greater and the quality suffers, any distance smaller and the quality improves.

download To receive information from an external source. This is usually done via a **modem**, retrieving information from a **Bulletin Board Service** (BBS) like CompuServe, but information can also be downloaded from a digital source, such as a digital camera, to a computer. The opposite term is *upload*.

DPI Dots per inch is a measurement of linear **resolution** for a **printer** or **scanner**. If a device has a resolution of 300 dpi it means that there are three hundred dots across and three hundred dots down. The tighter this cluster of dots is, the smaller the dot becomes. The higher the number of dots, the finer the **resolution**.

On a 300 dpi laser printer, there will be three hundred rows of dots in the space on one inch–a lot of dots. Some printers advertise resolution using two sets of numbers: For example, Fargo's Primera Pro printer features 600×300 resolution. In this case, the specifications indicate the horizontal and vertical resolutions. If you get your output printed on a Linotronic imagesetter, you can get 1200 dpi. If you thought your printed output looked good at 300 dpi, wait'll you see what it looks like at 1200 dpi.

But dpi ratings can sometimes fool you. Output from a 300 dpi dye-sublimation printers, because of the way they lay dots of colored dye on the paper–overlapping one another–can have a higher apparent resolution than say, a inkjet printer rated at 720 dpi. As in all forms of photography–digital or analog–your own eyes are the best test of whether any input or output peripheral meets you needs, regardless of its rated dpi.

draft mode The ability of a printer to produce output that has less than the highest quality a printer is capable of, approximating the original document or image. Draft mode is useful for when you are in a hurry and low-resolution output will provide enough information for viewing, reviewing, or correcting.

drag and drop This is a feature of Graphical User Interfaces (GUI) that lets users perform different operations by using the mouse to maneuver an icon representing files.

DRAM A propeller-head term for Dynamic Random Access Memory. DRAM cannot hold information for a long time and requires that the computer refresh the information ever few thousandths of a second–that's why it's called "dynamic." DRAM is the typical RAM chip that is found on SIMMs and, I guess, DIMMs too.

DVD Originally this meant Digital Video Disc, but with the development of a unified format has been changed to Digital *Versatile* Disc by some marketing mavens. Whether this oh-so-clever definition will remain is up to the marketplace.

In what promises to be a revolution in home electronics as well as computing, the DVD format, which utilizes a dual-layer technology to store more information that a standard CD-ROM disc, will bring increased storage capacity. Two versions are expected; one will be able to hold 2.6 GB (that's gigabytes) or 4.7GB. Keep an eye out for this format.

DXF Drawing Interchange Format, utilized by AutoCad's popular computer-aided drawing software package.

dye-sublimation Often called just "dye-sub" or **thermal dye-transfer**, this process is used in printers that use a printing head that heats a dye

Fargo Electronics Pictura 310 dye-sublimation printer is a 300 × 300 dpi printer that can use paper up to 12" × 20". The Pictura 310 can also output media using low-cost wax thermal ribbon and paper. The printer uses a parallel interface for connection to all Windows-based computers and Mac users (who lack this kind of interface) will find a NuBus parallel port bundled with their version of the printer.

ribbon creating a gas that hardens into a deposit on the special paper used by the printer. The more heat applied by the head, the denser the color and the denser the image on the paper will appear.

Like that of most printers, the output of printers using the dye-sub process appears in the form of "dots" of color, but because these dye spots are soft-edged (instead of the hard edges created by laser and inkjet printers), the result is smooth continuous tones. This makes dye-sub printers work especially well with photographs, and even 300 dpi dye-sub output can be striking.

When assessing the quality of printer output, digital photographers appear to be divided into two groups: The first is looking for an inexpensive printer that can deliver quality results. At this time, the Fargo Primera Pro (the company's $8^1/_2 \times 11$-inch, 300 dpi model) and Pictura printers are the best available solution. The second group is composed of photographers who want to be able to include "acceptable" looking photographs in their correspondence and newsletters. This second group will love the Epson family of Stylus color inkjet printers.

Remember the dye-sublimation process was originally designed as a proofing media, not to be used the final product. According to Fargo Electronics, dye-sublimation prints will not last as long as a properly processed color prints, but other than dye-transfer prints, most conventionally processed silver-based color prints have a limited life too. Dye-sub prints should have a long life, but like videotape, no one has yet done a definitive archival study. Deterioration of the image and color is mostly caused by exposure to ultraviolet radiation. The best advice is to store the print properly (cool, no direct light) and place it under ultraviolet protective glass. This glass, available at many framing shops, can reduce 99 percent of UV emissions. Yes, it is expensive. Also be sure to save a backup of the digital image using Photo CD or similar storage media.

TIP: On working with dye-sublimation printers like the Fargo Pictura. To avoid creating splotches or blobs on your prints later on, handle the ribbon by the edges. After placing the paper in the tray, make sure the side and back printer guides are snug. This is especially important to maintain registration, because the many of these printers make four passes—one for cyan, yellow, magenta, and black—of the paper when it prints an image in dye-sublimation mode. (Some dye-sub printers make only three passes, skipping the black step. This makes the process faster, but not necessarily better.) The first is through the yellow portion of the ribbon, the second through the magenta, the third through the cyan, and finally the black layer. Keeping the paper flat makes sure that the four passes are in perfect registration. During all the time I have had the dye-sub printer, I never had any serious registration problems.

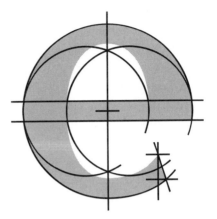

edit The process of changing or modifying a text, graphics, or image file.

e-mail Electronic mail. A technique for sending messages and even image files from place to place without using paper. To use e-mail you will need to have several things: First you need a **modem**. A modem converts an image file or message into a digital form that can be sent over telephone lines to a **BBS**, an **on-line service** like CompuServe, or the **Internet**. Through a monthly subscription to any of these services you can send e-mail across town or around the globe.

EIA The Electronic Industries Association is an organization of manufacturers that distributes electronic product interface and code standards to its members.

ELF Extremely Low Frequency radiation produced by computer monitors. *See* **EMF**.

EMF If you spend more than a few hours at your computer a day you should be aware of the controversy surrounding the potential problems caused by the Electromagnetic Fields (EMF) that computer monitors produce. All monitors emit some kind of Very Low Frequency (**VLF**) and Extremely Low Frequency (**ELF**) radiation, and color monitors emit more than monochromatic ones. A cathode-ray tube releases most of its radiation from the sides and back of the monitor. That's why it's a good idea to sit four or five feet away from your monitor. For most people that's not possible, but you should at least keep it at arm's length from you. You'll see screen filters that purport to block radiation from computer monitors, but even lead doesn't stop some ELF and VLF waves.

emulation The use of hardware or software to allow one type of computer to run programs written for another.

The Power Macintosh system software contains an emulation routine that allows programs written for older Macs to run on Power Macintoshes. Then there are ways that the Macintosh can be made to run programs produced for the PC.

With PCs using **SCSI** interfaces and Power Macintosh computers with PCI slots, the two competing platforms appear to be coming closer together. This seems even more possible because of the use of the PowerPC microprocessor chips by IBM and Apple. Are we approaching a computing nirvana? As I write this, the PowerPC consortium (IBM, Apple, and Motorola) is hinting that "in the winter of 1996" they will build a microprocessor chip called the 615 that will allow users to launch their computer as IBM-compatible, Macintosh, or both. Until that day comes, there are two readily available ways to allow one machine—an Apple Macintosh—to do the work of two.

Hardware emulation options include Apple's DOS-compatible card for the Power Macintosh and Reply Corporation's DOS On Mac card that fits non-Power Macintoshes and even some Performa models. Both use the computer's PDS (Processor Direct Slot). Recently there are rumors of two forthcoming (from Apple) DOS compatibility boards that will fit the new PCI-based Macs. The first PCI card is said to be powered by an Intel 486 chip running at either 66 or 100 MHz and is expected to be a $500 option for a Power Macintosh. The second board is expected to use a 60 or 90 MHz Pentium chip and is aimed at the higher-end PCI Power

Macintoshes because it cannot fit inside the smaller models. The Pentium-powered model is expected to cost $700.

At MacWorld Expo 95, Orange Micro introduced a MS-DOS Co-processor card that fits in any Macintosh with a NuBus slot. The MS-DOS Coprocessor supports 1,024 × 768 video with 256 colors on any Macintosh monitor, has serial and parallel ports, a PCMCIA slot, and 128K of cache memory for faster processing speeds and lets Mac users read DOS CD-ROM disks. Three models of the board are available, providing emulation of everything from a 486SX25 up to a 486 DX4/100 computer. All three solutions allow you to copy and paste text between the PC half of your computer and the Mac half, as well as share files on the Mac's hard disk. Orange Micro recently announced upgrades for Windows 95.

With the introduction of SoftWindows 2.0, Insignia Solutions offers a software-only solution to emulating the Windows environment on a Power Macintosh. Since SoftWindows is software, it doesn't tie up a PDS or NuBus slot and is less expensive. SoftWindows emulates an Intel 486 chip, and performance is scalable. The faster your Power Macintosh is, the faster SoftWindows will run. You can expect performance similar to a 25 MHz 486SX IBM-compatible. SoftWindows requires a 16MB computer, but all the Mac's RAM is available when the emulation isn't running, and you can use Apple's Virtual Memory or Connectix's RAM Doubler without problems. SoftWindows supports all Apple monitors and third-party monitors, like my NEC XE15, that work with the Mac and Windows machines. SoftWindows also provides full Windows sound support, but not Sound Blaster compatibility. Depending on your application, that may or may not be a problem. It didn't cause me any trouble.

If networking is a consideration, SoftWindows is fully network-aware when using Ethernet, Token Ring, and AppleTalk. SoftWindows 2.0 is the ideal solution for the Power Macintosh owner who needs to run one or a few PC-only products. Software emulation is inherently slower, albeit cheaper, than hardware emulation, and I've found SoftWindows is great for running a program like PhotoWorks Plus from Seattle FilmWorks. This Windows-only product runs slower on my Power Macintosh than on my 486 machine, but I am able to use the program with other Macintosh graphics programs and swap images between the two environments by copying images onto the Mac's clipboard and pasting into a Mac application. The same would be true for other Windows-only apps like

CorelDRAW!, Lotus Notes, and Novell's PerfectOffice. Insignia Solutions will be offering its own upgrade to Windows 95, but as I write this, it is not currently available. Also rumors abound that Connectix, creators of RAM Doubler, will be offering a Windows 95 environment for the Mac.

How 'bout Macintosh on an IBM? Here the picture gets fuzzier. IBM's standard hardware configuration for computers using the PowerPC chip is called the PowerPC Reference Platform, or **PReP**. Apple Computer did not buy into PReP, but has agreed to a later (and as yet unbuilt) specification called Common Hardware Platform, or CHRP. Apple has promised that its next operating system, code-named "Copland," will run on CHRP platforms regardless who builds them. In the meantime, a small Swiss company called Quix has been able to get Apple's System 7.5 up and running on a PReP-specification computer. *See* **PReP** for more information.

encrypt To protect the contents of a file or e-mail message from being read or seen by unauthorized people by converting the original data into a form that can only be read by someone who has the software "key." Military messages are routinely encrypted using various forms of "secret code." The Allied Enigma machine was the most famous code breaker in World War II. It translated encrypted messages into readable form. Confidential financial or business data needs to be similarly encrypted to protect against industrial espionage, while an e-mail message to your brother Michael may not have to be.

end user A term often used to describe the last person in the "food chain" of computer—beginning with the manufacturer of the product and ending with the actual person using that product.

EPROM Erasable Programmable Read-Only Memory chip. A chip that, unlike the CPU in your microcomputer, can be erased and reprogrammed or "burned." Many EPROMs are used to create **BIOS** chips.

EPS, EPSF Encapsulated PostScript format. A **metafile** format for graphics files that are designed to be imported into another application, such as a desktop publishing program. This type of file contains two elements: the bitmapped image and the PostScript code that tells your printer or output device how to print the image. *See* **PostScript**.

error message A message, often in the form of a **dialog box**, that tells a computer user that they have a problem. Sometimes, the message includes an onscreen button that you can click with your mouse and recover from the problem. Other times the error message may indicate a **bomb** or **crash**.

ESC The Escape key found on both Macintosh and PC computer keyboards. Some software programs use keyboard combinations (the simultaneous pressing of two or more keys) that use the ESC key to accomplish something. On a Macintosh running System 7.0 or later, holding the ESC-Option-Command keys can help you escape from a program that has locked up.

Ethernet A form of Local Area Network (LAN) that connects computers from different manufacturers (up to 1,024 computers) and enables them to communicate. Computers must have an interface card or have Ethernet capability built in (some recent Macs have this feature). Ethernet was developed jointly by Xerox, DEC, and Intel.

Ethertalk The name of software developed by Apple Computer that allows Macintosh computers to connect to Ethernet networks.

expansion board Often called just card or board. This is a circuit board that plugs into an **expansion slot** on the computer's **motherboard** to add increased functionality to the computer.

For a digital photographer, the graphics display card is the most important part of the computer system. The graphics card plugs into a slot on the motherboard and has a port that sticks out the back of the computer's case. This video port is the place where you plug a cable that connects the monitor with the card. Choosing the right graphics card is as important as a monitor. You can buy a 24-bit board but it may be limited in the amount of colors it can display by the **DRAM** (Dynamic Random Access Memory) chips it has installed. Good boards have either 2–4MB of DRAM or room to add more. Make sure the video board you buy has enough memory or can be expanded. In Macintosh systems, the video card function is built into the motherboard, but space is provided for **VRAM** (Video Random Access Memory) SIMMs to expand the quality of the video display.

Expansion boards, as their name implies, expand the capabilities of a computer. One of the most popular first boards installed in a PC is a sound card, like the Creative Lab's Sound Blaster card shown here.

Just as with interchangeable lenses, there are many kinds of cards manufactured by many different companies. Selecting the card to do the job you want is comparable to deciding which manufacturer's 35–70 mm lens you should add to your camera system. To find the right lens, you read product reviews in magazines and talk to your friends about their experience with theirs. Do the same thing with cards.

expansion slot On your computer's **motherboard** you'll see rows of plastic and metal strips that look as if they're designed to have something inserted into them. They are. They are called *expansion slots*, *bus slots*, or just plain *slots*, and accept printed circuit cards that allow accessories or devices to be attached to the motherboard. These cards are the computer equivalent of interchangeable camera lenses, and depending on what type of card or **expansion board** is inserted in the slot, these cards allow the computer to accomplish different tasks.

In order for input and output devices to function, they must be physically attached (by cables) to a card inserted into a slot. In the PC world, you will find 8-bit, 16-bit, and 32-bit slots and depending on the motherboard design, you will find one or two of each type of slot installed. One way to identify the different slots is that as they go from 8 to 16 to 32 bits, the slot gets longer. Inside a Macintosh you will find **NuBus** and **PDS** (Processor Direct Slot) slots. A NuBus card automatically tells the CPU what its function is, but a PDS slot is passive and is used for specific functions, like the board that allows the Macintosh to emulate the IBM-PC environment. Some cards have connectors that stick out the back of the computers. These are called **ports**, and allow different external devices, like printers, to be connected to them. There are many kinds of ports and slots for both PCs and Macs. The size and number of slots determine the expandability of your computer.

The slots in PC-compatible machines come in a wide variety of types. It is important you know what kinds of slots are on your motherboard, so you can install the appropriate, matching card. Here's a quick round-up of the types you're likely to find:

- **ISA**: These slots are the Industry Standard Architecture type you find in almost every PC, and the typical graphics card is designed for an ISA slot.
- **VL bus**: Stands for VESA Local Bus; VESA means Video Electronics Standard Association. VL bus cards will not work in an ISA slot.
- **PCI local bus**: Personal Computer Interconnect is the faster successor to the VL bus, and often will sit alongside an ISA slot on a motherboard. Until recently, PCI slots were limited to IBM-compatible machines. In the latest generation of Power Macintosh computers, Apple Computer abandoned their NuBus slot architecture in favor of the PCI bus.
- **MCA**: Micro-Channel Architecture is found only on some IBM-brand PS/2 machines and in few others.
- **ACCESS bus**: Provides two-way communications between peripherals and the CPU. ACCESS bus eliminates the need to install complex files or **drivers** by having the inserted card communicate directly with the CPU to identify the board's function(s).
- **PNP**: Plug-and-Play slots are similar to the ACCESS bus in their ability to communicate and allow the computer to recognize any card inserted into it though exchange of information.

exposure index (Not really a digital imaging term but provided here for those non-photographer who have to deal with digital images and have inquiring minds.) In the most basic terms, *exposure index* is the number you set on your light meter or film to expose a specific film and *may be different* than the rated ISO speed provided by the manufacturer. The way that an *exposure index* is arrived at is by testing specific film emulsions under real-world conditions.

For example, in my own studio I used the following test to determine the exposure index for Kodak's T-Max 100 film. The same procedure can be used with any film—color or black and white, negative or transparency—regardless of format. The camera used was a Hasselblad EL/M with 150 mm lens attached and lighting was supplied by Bogen and Courtenay monolights. I started by loading an A-12 back with a roll of Kodak T-MAX 100 film. My subject held a Macbeth Color Checker with a 3M Post-It note attached listing the lens and aperture used for each exposure. Starting by making exposures at one stop less than the flash meter showed, I bracketed at half stops until two stops over the indicated aperture. I did the same thing with two different 150 mm lenses and sent the film to our lab with instructions to select the best negative and make a 5×7 print from it. When I got the test print back, it was (technically) the best black-and-white print I'd seen in a long time. The tests showed the best negatives were produced between f/11 and f/8, which suggests an *exposure index* of 50 for T-MAX 100. Kodak's official ISO rating was, of course, 100. Your lab may use different materials and processing systems, so please use my results as a basis for conducting your own tests.

extensions (1) For Macintosh, see **INIT**. (2) For IBM: In DOS and Windows, file names are divided into two parts. The first part (before the period) is the file name, and the extension (after the period) indicates the kind of file it is. A DINO.BMP file identifies the file as a bitmapped graphic. **BMP** is the acronym for Windows bitmap graphic file. Please note that there are extensions for text files as well as graphics files.

external device If an internal device is a peripheral, such as a **CD-ROM** drive that is built into the computer's case, an external device is a peripheral that is outside the computer's case and connected to it via a cable to one of the **ports** on the back of the computer. Many external devices are used for storage, such as **removable media** drives.

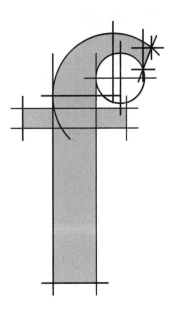

FAQ Frequently Asked Questions. A term, often found on **Internet** home pages, that will lead you to an area containing the most frequently asked questions that visitors to the web site may have.

fatware Computer slang for those large, overweight programs that consume more RAM and more **hard disk** space than the previous version of the same program did.

file This is a collection of data saved and named as an individual entity, that is also occasionally referred to as a document. Your computer views files as a collection of bytes of data. Each program creates a unique file type that is readable only by that program or compatible programs. Adobe Photoshop, for example, saves image files in a format readable only by Adobe Photoshop (and those other programs that read this format) but also gives you the option of saving the file in a generic graphics format like **TIFF**.

file conversion

file conversion The process of converting one file type, typically from one platform, to another file type for another platform, as from Windows to Macintosh. While some graphics programs have a limited ability to read files from other platforms, file conversions usually require specialized software to perform the required translation. Here's a quick overview of how it works:

There are dozens of different types of PC and Windows files and bunches more for the Macintosh. Graphic file incompatibilities affect many computer users, none more than the digital imager or desktop publisher. For example, my pal Barry produces a client newsletter with his Mac IIci, and a PC-using friend wants to give him clip art to use in the next edition. Another friend, Christy, is creating a brochure for a non-profit organization using her Gateway PC, and asks me to scan images for it using my Macintosh. Both of these people need to convert files from the world of DOS and Windows to that of the Macintosh or vice versa, but transformations sometimes need to be made for graphics on the same platform.

Understanding what a file acronym means takes some of the stress out of starting the conversion process. Inside these pages you'll find definitions for common graphics files, but unless you have the right power tools, managing these conversions can be frustrating. The key to success is choosing a utility that accomplishes what you want with the least amount of fuss and the least amount of cost. The next step is determining how intense your needs are by analyzing what file types and platforms are involved.

When converting files between Macintosh and PC computers, it helps if you have software that allows your computer to read (or mount) disks that were formatted on the "other" machine. Apple's Macintosh PC Exchange 2.0 lets Macintosh and compatible computers read and write disks that were formatted on IBM-compatible machines, as well as disks created on Apple II computers. (This might help you with the latter computers which are still used in some K–12 education environments.) The latest version of the software recognizes DOS SCSI hard disk and removable media drives, such as Bernoulli and SyQuest. In addition to allowing your Macintosh to read and format DOS disks, Macintosh PC Exchange provides file conversion directly from the desktop. For example, a .PCX file can be preset to open as a Macintosh PICT file, and can be opened just by double clicking the DOS file's icon. Macintosh PC

Exchange is included with Apple's System 7.5 operating system and is frequently bundled with software for Performa computers sold in computer discount stores. DataViz, for example, packages PC Exchange as part of their MacLink Plus 8.0 package.

On the other side of the cross-platform issue, DataViz's MacOpener for Windows lets users of PC compatibles read and write Macintosh floppy disks, as well as SCSI-based removable media drives (like Iomega's Zip) and CD-ROM discs. When running MacOpener with Windows 95, the full file name is retained when you move files from the Mac disk onto the PC's hard disk. Users can also preview Mac text and graphics files (in either EPS or PICT formats) before copying them onto the disk. When using Windows 3.1, the full Mac file name is retained, instead of the truncated names limited by DOS.

Because the competition for this kind of utility is slim, Macintosh owners have a simpler time selecting the right conversion program. Adobe Photoshop comes closest to being a universal graphics file translator, but its high price makes it useful only if you already need a photo-enhancement program. MacLink Plus, on the other hand, is a better choice for the average Mac user. DataViz claims their latest version supports 550 file translation combinations, but most of them are word processing, database, and spreadsheet formats. The good news is that DataViz's implementation of Apple's Easy Open concept makes any file conversion as easy as double-clicking a file. With its reasonable price and ease of use, MacLink Plus can't be beat.

Windows users have more choices, but finding the right program can be confusing. There are three contenders for best value in mid-range Windows conversion utilities. Here they are in inverse order according to price: Conversion Artist imports thirty-two different formats and views and saves in seventeen. It's a no-frills conversion package with an exceptionally well-written and concise user's manual. Its interface is ho-hum and its overall value is eclipsed by DeltaPoint's FreezeFrame.

FreezeFrame imports and exports fewer file types than Conversion Artist, but features a graphical user interface and a price almost half that of the other program. FreezeFrame uses a modular construction: FF Viewer displays any graphics file the program supports, and you can access its conversion utility—FF Convert—from within Viewer. The program includes a screen capture utility called FF Capture, and FF Icon Editor for those Windows users who like to play with their icons.

In addition to image conversion (in batches if you like), Paint Shop Pro performs rudimentary image editing, does screen captures, and supports **TWAIN**-compliant scanners.

When the conversion gets tough, I reach for Equilibrium Systems' DeBabelizer for the Mac and Inset System's HiJaack 95 for my Windows 95 computer. Both programs do more than convert file formats, but HiJaack 95 does a lot more. It can view over seventy different graphic file formats, and even provides image enhancement capabilities. HiJaack 95 provides screen capture from either DOS or Windows, and includes image-management capability. Compared to HiJaack 95, the interface of DeBabelizer is mundane, but the program's powerful scripting features allows users to convert large numbers of files into a single format. This could be very handy if you were collecting a variety of graphics that would be included in a **CD-ROM** and wanted to maintain the same format and approximate file size.

Most Windows-based programs are biased in favor of converting more DOS and Windows formats than Macintosh files. The same is true of Macintosh conversion programs. Keep this in mind when you're trying to pound a square file into a round hole. The only solution for the "impossible" file conversion may be to call up the file using the application that created it and save the file in a more "portable" format. As a last resort, you can take the file to a **service bureau**, and for a modest fee the company will usually be able to covert the file into a format you can use.

file protection A means of protecting a file from being erased or overwritten. On a 3½-inch **floppy disk** this is accomplished by sliding the write-protect tab (located in the upper left-hand corner on the back of the disk) from closed to open. Most system software also has provisions to allow a file on your **hard disk** or **removable media** to be similarly protected.

film recorder Also called **CFR** or Color Film Recorder. A desktop film recorder is essentially a camera enclosed in a small box and focused on a very high-resolution black-and-white monitor. The CFR makes three exposures of the image through separate red, blue, and green filters to produce the final image. If this sounds slow to you—it can be.

Not many photographers purchase or use film recorders. You'll find most of them in **service bureaus**. One reason for this is that they've

Polaroid's HR6000 24-bit film recorder can be used to turn your digital images into slides. In addition to 35 mm film, the HR6000 supports twenty different kinds of film and offers interchangeable backs including Polaroid Instant Film and 4 × 5 sheet film.

typically been designed to meet the needs of people producing slide presentations, not photographs. The image-making needs of these two groups are quite different, and presenters are less inclined to go ballistic than the typical photographer if a photograph used in a chart is slightly off-color.

Keep in mind that using a film recorder introduces two more variables into your **color management system**: the emulsion of the film used, and how that film is processed. If you are one of those photographers who have used slide duplicators from companies like Pentax, Bessler, and Bogen to make slide dupes and enjoy working with various filters and contrast reduction methods to produce the "perfect" dupe slide, you're ready for desktop film recorders. In truth, working with a film recorder is easier than using a slide duplicator, but a similar mindset is required.

To help you evaluate which kind of CFR you should purchase, here are a few rules of thumb:

- *Resolution*: Select a CFR that offers at least 24-bit images and 16 million colors, and has 4,000 lines of resolution. This way, the output will have excellent clarity and sharpness, along with smoothly ramped continuous tones and accurate color.
- *Affordabilty*: Match the film recorder to your budget. According to respected photo industry publication, *The Hope Report*, slides generated with in-house film recorders typically cost about 55¢ each, with the cost of the CFR amortized over two years. Service Bureau slides, while they have an oft-quoted $6 to $7 per slide cost, have an actual cost of $29.18 each because of the number of remakes often required to "get it right." You need to balance your needs with the cost of the film recorders, which start at $6,000 and go up from there. Choose a CFR that is compatible with both Mac and Windows as well as providing network support. This will make it easy for you to adapt to a new system if you decide to change platforms or choose to sell the film recorder later on. At the same time, make sure the CFR has true "plug-and-play" capabilities to make it easy to install and operate as well as portable.
- *Versatility*: Make sure the film recorder has removable backs. This will give you the flexibility of using 35 mm slide or negative film, as well as using sheet film or Polaroid prints film for an instant proof.

film scanner *See* **scanner**.

filter (1) A hardware device that separates specific signals or data from an electronic signal or groups of data.

(2) A **plug-in** that is added to your graphics or image-enhancement program to produce a special effect within user-definable parameters. Special effects, similar to what can be achieved with modular camera filter systems, are also possible with digital filters when used with image-enhancement programs, like Adobe Photoshop. Instead of screwing these filters onto the front of your lens, all you need to do is copy them into Adobe Photoshop's "Plug-Ins" folder and they'll appear within the program's Filter menu. One of the first digital filter packages available was Aldus (now Adobe) Gallery Effects, and it remains one of my favorites. Other popular filter packages include MetaTool's **Kai's Power Tools**. For more information on filters, see **plug-ins**.

fixed disk Another name for **hard disk**. A fixed disk is a permanent part of a drive mechanism, as opposed to **removable media** drives that have cartridges which can be removed and replaced.

flat panel A monitor or display that uses LCD (Liquid Crystal Display) technology instead of a CRT (Cathode-Ray Tube) used in conventional monitors. Since the screen is perfectly flat (unlike a rounded CRT) they are often called *flat screen displays*. Advantages: smaller desktop space requirements and less heat generated. Disadvantages: higher cost and slower screen redraw, although these two are diminishing with each new generation of flat screen displays.

flatbed plotter Sometimes just called *plotter*. This is a computer printer that uses a group of pens, each one filled with a different colored ink, to produce **CAD** drawings typically used in engineering and architectural applications.

floppy disk This is a round, thin disk coated with the same kind of ferrous oxide used on audio cassette tape. The disk is encapsulated in an almost square protective shell with a sliding gate (or shutter) that opens a slot in the shell that allows the drive to read or write onto the magnetic material.

In the old days, 8-inch floppy disks were the only size and they really were floppy. Then the 5¼-inch floppy disks used by Apple II and early IBM PCs were introduced and 8-inch disks disappeared, except for some rare applications. Each of these 5¼-inch disks held 360K of data, but when Apple introduced the Macintosh, they delivered it with a drive that used 3½-inch disks encapsulated in plastic, making them, well, less floppy. Needless to say, computer types, being the kind of people we are, still call them floppy disks.

Today's floppy disks come in several flavors. Some PCs use both 5¼-inch 1.2MB and 3½-inch 1.44MB drives, while Macintosh has standardized on 3½-inch 1.44MB drives. The 3½-inch disks used in recent Macs or PCs hold 1.44MB of data. Older versions held 720K (800K on a Mac), so new disks carry the designation "high-density." Since most PC software is now being delivered on 3½-inch disks (or CD-ROM), you really don't need a 5¼-inch drive for your computer unless you're the kind of person who likes to wear a belt *and* suspenders.

Since photographic image files are usually quite large, they seldom fit on a single floppy disk. One exception to this rule is the Pictures On Disk service offered by Seattle FilmWorks.

floppy disk drive The floppy drive is an input and/or output device and is connected to the motherboard. Inside the drive is a read/write head that acts much like the arm of a phonograph turntable, except that instead of being fixed, it can move in and out to find data or write data onto the disk.

"flying toasters" One of the most popular screen savers for the Macintosh or Windows machines is Berkeley Systems' After Dark. One of the original modules is called *Flying Toasters* in which old-fashioned, winged, toasters fly across the screen, accompanied by flying slices of toast. The latest version of the software includes music, including a karaoke version. Flying Toasters is proof that computer users like to have fun too.

font The short definition is that fonts are a group of type characters that are related by style and size, but there's much more to font and font management than that.

My friend Karen is part of a vanishing breed: a traditional typesetter. She told me it always bothered her that computer users used the terms *font* and *typeface* interchangeably, when it fact they were not. A "typeface," she pointed out, "refers only to the shape and design of the characters, not their size." Helvetica, for example, is a typeface. "A font," she corrected me, "is a collection of a certain typeface in a specific size." Ten-point Helvetica, therefore, is a font. Unless you're speaking with a printer and are confusing them with your usage of *font* and *typeface*, it doesn't make too much difference which term you use.

Computer fonts come in two basic varieties: **bitmapped** and outline, with variations on each of these categories. The original Macintosh fonts were bitmapped or "screen" fonts and were made up of a series of dots that have the same resolution (72 dots per inch) as the Mac's screen. That's where the term *screen font* comes from. Bitmapped fonts are often named after cities; my original Mac came with New York, Geneva, London, and San Francisco fonts, among others. Screen fonts come in specific sizes, which are shown in the Font or Size menu of your word processor or desktop publishing program. If you select a point size that is not installed in your System Folder, your computer will try to interpolate the size you requested from the sizes that are installed. If you only have a few font sizes of a given typeface installed, this can look pretty jaggy, especially when printed with a **dot-matrix** printer.

To get around these limitations, Adobe introduced the concept of outline fonts, using a technology called **PostScript**. Type 1 PostScript fonts are outline font programs based on the PostScript language, and contain "hints." Hints are the process of adding information to a character's outline to improve its appearance at low resolution and small point sizes. Type 3 PostScript fonts lack the hinting contained in Type 1. Nevertheless, they're useful for complex shapes, like logos. Adobe's Type 1 outline fonts are "scalable" fonts, the computer stores a mathematical representation of each font which can be scaled up or down without getting a bad case of the jaggies when printed. PostScript fonts come in pairs: a bitmapped screen font that's used onscreen and a *printer* font that will be used to image the font on your printer.

To print PostScript fonts you'll need a PostScript printer, which are usually more expensive than non-PostScript printers. Since not all printers can handle PostScript fonts, Adobe developed **ATM** (Adobe Type Manger). ATM lets you print PostScript fonts on non-PostScript printers. If you don't have or can't afford a PostScript printer, get a copy of ATM. Most PostScript printers have printer fonts built-in, and the manufacturers include a disk of the screen versions of these fonts. These built-in fonts are called "resident" fonts. The typical resident fonts are Avant Garde, Bookman, Courier, Helvetica, New Century Schoolbook, Palatino, Symbol (Has anyone found a real use for this font?), Times, Zapf Chancery, and Zapf Dingbats. If it's not built-in, like one of my favorites, Tekton, you'll have to install both screen and printer elements so your printer can download the font to print your document. That's why you'll hear this class of fonts called "downloadable" fonts. Once a font gets big enough to stand out as a headline or title, it's called a "display" font. Traditional typesetters have always called any font bigger than 14 points a display font.

TrueType is an attempt to introduce inexpensive scalable font technology into the Macintosh and Windows operating environments. TrueType fonts look good on screen, and when output from either a PostScript or non-PostScript printer. Unlike PostScript fonts, TrueType fonts have only one component and have a slightly different icon so you won't get them confused with bitmapped fonts. To muddy the font waters,

font

Adobe introduced the Multiple Master Typeface series of Type 1 fonts. Multiple Master fonts let you generate variations on a font to fit a particular need. You can expand or condense, optically size, and fine-tune the font's appearance by using a Control Panel that lets you change a font's weight (thickness), width, and size.

Like many people, you will probably end up with a Fonts folder full of all three types of fonts, with Adobe Type Manager installed for good measure. If so, you might be worried that if you have several versions of the same typeface installed it could create some kind of conflict. Fear not. For on-screen use, your computer will use a bitmapped font, providing it's been installed in the proper size. Otherwise, it'll look for a TrueType version of the font. If you've got ATM installed, it will pick a PostScript font, and if necessary, adjust a bitmapped font to make it work. When printing on non-PostScript printers, the computer first selects a TrueType font, then the Postscript font as handled by ATM. If all fails it will scale up (or down) a bitmapped font. The old trick of having a font installed at twice the size used still works here, but will never look as crisp as using an outline font. When printing on a PostScript printer, the resident fonts will be used first, then your computer will look into the printer's RAM to see if a downloadable font is present. If nothing's there, it will look on the printer's hard disk (if it has one), then finally in the Extensions or Fonts folder (or directory). If that sounds confusing, don't worry about it unless you have a problem.

The scene has changed a lot since those early days when fonts were so expensive you felt like you had to tuck them in and kiss them good night. Led by Apple and Microsoft's attempts to make fonts part of the system software, prices have plummeted as new companies have burst on the scene with inexpensive clones of popular fonts. That's the good news. The bad news is that with the proliferation of fonts you need to make sure that you maintain standards.

Let me explain. You're using the Bookman typeface in a newsletter and proof it on your laser printer. Then you take the file to a print shop or service bureau to have it imaged at 1,200 dpi. When you get it back, you discover that the type looks like Bookman, but the spacing, line breaks, and size of the letters look different from what you printed in your office. Some words could even be cut off. Although TrueType fonts match Adobe's Type 1 PostScript font metrics (shapes) exactly, it may not match another font-maker's implementation of the same font. Most larger service bureaus have hundreds of fonts, but not all small print shops will. If you're not doing the imagesetting yourself, take the time to check what kind of fonts the company doing the work for you has installed. Make sure to provide a proof print and ask whoever's imaging your project to call if it doesn't look the same. This incompatibility can even affect you if you're bringing work home to print on your home machine.

FPU Floating Point Unit. A chip that handles a computer's floating point operations and can quickly calculate a large range of numbers. In floating point arithmetic, digits are stored in two parts: the *mantissa,* and the location of the decimal point called the *exponent.* Floating point math can be implemented by hardware with a FPU chip (or math coprocessor) or it can be done with software. The FPU chip is the faster approach. In the past, these chips were physically separate from the CPU. With the advent of the PowerPC and Pentium chips, FPUs are often built into the main CPU chip.

fractal A graphics term originally defined by mathematician Benoit Mandelbrot to describe a category of geometric shapes characterized by an irregularity in shape and design.

freeware A form of **shareware** that is just what it sounds like—it's free.

friction feed A method of moving paper (in printers) by use of rubber rollers in much the same manner as was done in a typewriter.

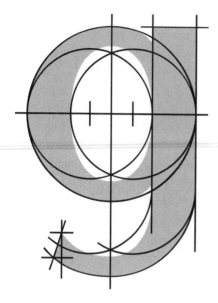

game port A **port** on the back of a computer that allows users to connect joysticks, steering wheels, and other controller devices used with games. Some multi-function expansion boards offer a game port.

gamma All photographs have a characteristic called *gamma*. The amount of gamma present in an image is measured as the contrast that affects the midlevel grays (the midtones) of an image. The good news for digital imagers is that this gamma is totally adjustable by most image-enhancement programs, and you aren't stuck with the gamma present in the original negative or print. I wonder what Ansel Adams would say about that?

gamut Every output device (e.g., a printer or monitor) has a range of colors that it can accurately reproduce. This range is called the *gamut* of the device. Every device from every manufacturer, whether it is a monitor or printer, has a unique gamut. Each device's gamut is part of a standard area of color science called "color space," and different types of devices work in different color spaces. Because of the way they are designed and constructed, monitors work in a different color space than printers do and this creates part of the problem that is color management. If you find that the output of your color printer doesn't match what you see on screen, you are beginning to understand the need for color management. The display is "in gamut" for the monitor, but not the printer. The problem is compounded by the fact that the gamuts of desktop devices, not unlike film itself, is relatively small when compared to the spectrum of visible light.

gas plasma screen Some **flat panel** screens use gas plasma—a design that uses neon and argon gases—to create a flicker-free screen. Glass plasma screens require less power and have long life but are (currently) more expensive than the conventional **CRT** design.

GB Gigabyte. A billion **bytes** or (more correctly) 1,024 megabytes.

GHz Gigahertz. A measurement of frequency at one billion cycles per second.

GIF (Pronounced like the peanut butter.) The Graphics Interchange Format developed by CompuServe is completely platform-independent; the same bitmapped file created on a Macintosh is readable by a Windows graphics program. A GIF file is automatically compressed, and consequently takes up less space on your **hard disk**. Because some image and graphics programs consider GIF files to be **indexed color**, not all software read and write GIF files, but many do.

The future of the GIF format, at this time, is uncertain. When CompuServe developed the format, it used the Lempel-Ziv-Welch (LZW) compression algorithms as part of the design believing this technology to be in the public domain. As part of an acquisition, UNISYS (formerly Univac computers) gained legal rights to LZW, and a legal battle has ensued. The way it stands now, reading and possessing GIF files (or any other graphics file containing LZW-compressed images) is not illegal, but writing software which creates GIF (or other LZW based files) may be.

grabber hand An onscreen pointer used by graphics programs—and even plug-ins such as Second Glance Software's Chromassage—that looks like a hand and is used to select objects on screen.

graphic Any image, computer-generated or not. A logo is a graphic, and so is a photograph. Any software program that works with drawings or photographs is usually referred to as a graphics program.

graphics coprocessor A chip that performs much of the processing required to display graphics on a video screen and frees the CPU from the drudgery of repetitive drawing tasks. This is accomplished by directly intercepting commands to perform these operations and executing them on a coprocessor installed on the graphics expansion board, instead of the already overworked CPU. A graphics coprocessor speeds up the computer and increases productivity if you're running Microsoft Windows, or any screen-intensive software such as Adobe Photoshop or drawing programs like CorelDRAW!

graphics display For a digital photographer, the graphics display is the most important part of the computer system and consists of two parts: the graphics controller (or graphics **expansion card**) and the monitor. The graphics card plugs into a bus slot on the **motherboard** and has a video port that sticks out the back of the computer's case. The video port is the place where you plug a cable that connects the monitor with the card.

   Choosing the right graphics card is as important as a monitor. You can buy a 24-bit board, but it may be limited in the amount of colors in can display by the DRAM (Dynamic Random Access Memory) chips it has installed. Good boards have either 2 to 4MB of DRAM or room to add more. Make sure the video board you buy has enough memory or can be expanded. In Macintosh systems, the video card function is built into the motherboard, but space is provided for VRAM (Video Random Access Memory) SIMMs to expand the quality of the video display.

graphics tablet Graphics tablets have been around since the late sixties and are widely used in the **CAD**, computer graphics, and teleconferencing industries. Graphics tablets are often called *digitizing tablets* because they can convert film images, graphics, and drawings into digital information. This now-digitized visual data can be entered into the computer for storage, analysis, modification, or archiving.

graphics tablet

Long considered the province of the artist or designer, there are three reasons you should you be using a graphics tablet for digital imaging. First, because a stylus, or pen, is more natural to hold than a mouse, graphics tablets are one of the best ways to create non-text information. Second, the human engineering aspects of graphics tablets can, for some people, reduce the pain caused by carpal tunnel syndrome. Lastly, graphics tablets are a much more accurate pointing and input device than a mouse.

While the product is referred to as a tablet, they really have two major parts: tablet and pen, or stylus, that is used to "draw" on the tablet's sensitive surface. The tablet portion, which nowadays can be so thin as to be called a "pad," contains a mechanism for sensing where a stylus is positioned on the surface. The tablet bed contains a high-resolution matrix that can respond to active or passive actions. (Active response is when the element is drawn and passive is after it is drawn.) Digital information is represented as the x-y coordinates of where the pen is placed. The performance quality of graphics tablets is defined by resolution, accuracy, and linearity.

- *Resolution*: Measures the number of points per inch that a tablet can recognize and how fine a distinction it can make between adjacent points. Typical resolutions vary from 25 to 1,000 points per inch but specifications for high-end CAD markets are higher. Higher resolution devices cost more, but tablets can cost as little as $129 or more than $2,400 from the same manufacturer, depending on resolution and pad size.

- *Accuracy*: Measures fidelity to the actual distance being measured versus what happens on screen. A tablet that resolves 100 points per inch typically has an accuracy of 0.01 inches, and units that resolve 1,000 points per inch can exceed 0.005 inches of accuracy. By comparison, a human eye resolves approximately 5000 lines per inch at 10 inches. The average user's accuracy will be plus or minus 0.01 inches, but a skilled CAD operator can usually beat this.

- *Linearity*: Tells you how much variability there is in the first two parameters across your field of work.

Graphics tablets come in many configurations. The first variable is the tablet's size, which varies from 4×5 inches up to 44×60 inches, depending on the manufacturer and your specific application. When manufacturers specify size they are referring to the active area of the tablet; that is, its usable area and not the unit's physical size. A tablet's actual size is always slightly larger. One of the advantages of a flexible tablet is that it can be rolled out on any surface and left in place, acting not just as a tablet but as a permanent desktop or work area.

Styluses are available in several flavors, included both corded and cordless models. Cordless models are further subdivided by those that require batteries and those that do not. Each of these configurations has their advantages and disadvantages. Corded pens may be less convenient than cordless models but because they are tethered to the tablet with an umbilical you'll never lose a stylus. Another advantage of corded styluses is that they are always less expensive. Some pens feature the latest hot button features: erasablity and pressure sensitivity. To erase work, you can activate the erasing function by pressing one of the two buttons on the side of the pen, instead of having to flip the pen over to activate. A pressure-sensitive stylus lets you control the width of each pen stroke. The harder you rub, the more you erase.

Anything you can do with a mouse, you can do with a stylus. And there are some things a stylus does better. Try writing your name with a mouse, and you'll see what I mean. One area of stylus superiority is cursor placement. Instead of rolling a mouse to locate a cursor, just tap the pen on the tablet and that's where the cursor appears.

grayscale Refers to a series of gray tones ranging from white to pure black. The more shades or levels of gray, the more accurately an image will look like a full-toned black-and-white photograph. Most scanners will scan from 16 to 256 gray tones. A grayscale image file is typically one-third the size of a color one.

grayscale monitor Any monitor or LCD computer screen (on laptops) capable of displaying several shades of gray. A true black-and-white monitor can only display two tones: black or white.

green book *See* CD-ROM.

green PC A term used to refer to any energy-saving computer or peripheral. After a certain period of inactivity, "green" devices go into a suspended mode: Monitors go black to save phosphors and CPU's slow down to save power. The "green" concept also carries over to the type of packaging materials used in shipping computer equipment and includes extensive use of recycled and recyclable materials.

groupware This term applies to any program designed for use on a network, serving a group of users working on a related project.

The most popular groupware program is Lotus Notes. It was so popular that IBM purchased the company for 3.5 billion dollars just to get control of Notes.

GUI Graphical User Interface. A term probably originated at Xerox's PARC (Palo Alto Research Center). GUIs lets users use a pointing device, such as a mouse, to select objects on the screen to get the computer to achieve a desired result. Up till the Xerox Star, the command-line interface (as exemplified, but by no means originated by Microsoft's MS-DOS) was the only way to communicate with computers. If you wanted the computer to do anything, you needed to type a command in precisely defined terms. Leave out a comma or period or forget to capitalize a letter and you got an error message. A graphical user interface was developed by Xerox for their never-produced Star computer. Instead of a command line, the Star's interface required the use of a mouse to click on little pictures, called icons, to make the computer do what you wanted. The Macintosh popularized this approach to computers, which was followed several years later by Microsoft Windows.

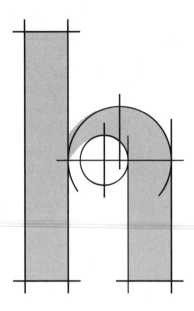

hacker Originally the term referred to those obsessed and talented computer users who create insanely great software for the sheer joy of it. Now the term has a pejorative meaning for those malicious misfits who create computer viruses or use their skills to break into other people's computer records.

half-duplex A term used in data transmission to describe a circuit that sends your data first in one direction (to the source), then back to you. A half-duplex circuit cannot transmit data in both directions simultaneously, but a full-duplex one can.

halftone The simulation of a continuous-tone image created with a dot pattern. Almost all printing processes print by using dots. In traditional, photographically generated halftones, a special-purpose graphics arts camera is used to photograph the original image through a halftone screen, which reproduces the image in dots by using smaller dots for lighter areas and larger dots for darker areas. But many digital printers are limited to only one dot size. To simulate varying size dots, computer printers use a **dithering** process that creates clusters of dots in cells. The more dots that are printed in a cell, the darker the gray tone appears.

halo When using a selection tool in an image-enhancement program to select certain kinds of objects, a *halo* may appear around part of that selection. These extra pixels are caused by the program's anti-aliasing feature. (Sometimes when a graphic is displayed on a monitor, you'll see jagged edges around some objects. These rough edges are caused by an effect called aliasing. Techniques that smooth out the **jaggies** are called anti-aliasing.) Most image enhancement programs have a built-in anti-aliasing function that partially blurs pixels on the fringe of a selection and causes additional pixels to be pulled into the selection. The best way to eliminate these "halo" pixels is by using the Defringe command found in the Matting submenu of the Select menu. Before you can apply it, however, the selection must be "floating." To make it float, select Float from the Select menu. Then you may safely select Defringe. When you do, a dialog appears asking how may pixels wide you want to Defringe. Typically you will only need to Defringe one pixel wide, but depending on the image, you may want to slightly increase the pixel width.

handshake A series of protocols that occurs when you use your modem to connect to a **BBS** or **on-line service**, like CompuServe. It's simply a method for both sending and receiving modems to verify that they are speaking the same language, and prevents the transmission of garbled data.

hard disk A computer's hard disk consists of one or more rigid (hard), non-flexible disks. Like the **floppy disk drive**, it has a read/write head, or multiple heads on multi-disk drives. Once data is written to it, you can think of your hard drive as a file cabinet that holds all the data inside your computer. Like a file cabinet, you can access this data whenever you want, and it's still there after you shut the computer down. (You never turn a computer off, it is always "shut down.") The capacity of hard disks is measured in megabytes, but unlike the 1.44MB that's standard for floppy disks, hard drives come in many different and larger sizes. Any computer

An inside look at a Conners Peripherals 3.5-inch hard disk. A hard disk is an electronic filing cabinet that stores all of your computer program's data, programs, and images. Unlike RAM, which loses data when power is lost, the data on your hard disk is ready and waiting when you turn your computer on.

you buy will already have a floppy drive and hard disk installed, and until you outgrow the hard drive (which will be sooner than you think) you won't have to worry about replacing it. In the early days of personal computing, a 20MB drive was standard, but this quickly changed to 100MB, and now anything smaller than 500MB is unacceptable for digital imaging. Fortunately, prices of hard disks have dropped as fast as the need for greater capacity has grown.

hardware Hardware is the physical (hard) combination of components that let a computer compute—the actual, physical computing machinery. On a modern autofocus camera, for example, the LCD display panel on top that shows aperture and shutter speed is part of the camera's hardware, but it's the camera's software that tells that display what F-stop the lens is set on and what shutter speed has been selected.

HDCD High-Density Compact Disc. A new CD-ROM format, based on the unified Digital Video Disc format, that is capable of storing 2.6 or 4.7GB. *See* **CD-ROM** for more details.

HDTV High-Definition Television. A typical TV set contains 336,000 pixels, while a high-definition TV set is expected to produce at least 2 million pixels. One standard recommends doubling the current 525 lines per picture to 1,050 lines, and increasing the screen aspect ratio from the current 12:9 to 16:9, which would result in a picture shaped more like a wide-screen movie. There are HDTV monitors that produce an amazingly lifelike appearance but not without some cost. Expect to pay in the neighborhood of $10,000.

head Sometimes called read/write head. This is an electronic device (not unlike a phonograph arm) that is found on all drives—**CD-ROM**, **floppy**, **hard**, or **removable media**—and can read and (usually) write information onto the medium.

head crash A hardware failure in which the read/write head comes in contact with the disk surface. This almost always results in loss of data. Because of the floating head design of Iomega's Bernoulli box drive, head crashes are extremely rare with that type of mechanism.

heap This is a programming term that refers to the pool of free memory (**RAM**) that is available for a program. You'll hear Mac-heads referring to the "system heap." This is the amount of free memory that is available for the Macintosh operating system.

Hercules graphics This is one of the original graphics standards for the IBM-PC, introduced in 1982 by Hercules Computer Technology. It quickly became the standard for all **monochrome** PC monitors. Hercules Graphics had 720 × 348 pixel resolution and used 64K of screen memory, but was never adopted as a color standard.

hertz It's not the rental car company, but hertz with a small *h*. Often abbreviated as Hz, this is the **ANSI** standard measure of frequency: electrical vibrations per second. Those of us around from the old days of radio remember the term as "cps" or cycles per second.

HFS Hierarchical Filing System. Used by the Apple Macintosh to format hard disks and identify the files on that disk and their location.

high color Sometimes called True Color. This is the ability of a PC's video expansion board and monitor to generate 16-bit color (65,536 color shades). Sometimes this also refers to 15-bit color, which, because it uses five bits for each red, green, and blue pixel, can only produce 32,768 colors. In 16-bit systems, the sixteenth bit can be a color, such as 5-red, 6-green, and 5-blue.

high memory (For IBM-compatible systems only.) Refers to **RAM** in the part of the first megabyte called the Upper Memory Area (**UMA**), in that part of the computer's memory between 640K and 1MB, or memory that exceeds 1MB, called extended memory. It can also refer to the 64K area between 1,024K and 1,088K, usually referred to as High Memory Area, or **HMA**. All this confusion about memory and the allocation of memory was supposed to disappear with Microsoft Windows 95, which could address however much RAM a user had installed, much in the same way that the Macintosh operating system does.

high res High-Resolution. More information (or pixels) filling your screen means that images will appear in finer detail, with smoother edges. For instance: in Kodak's Photo CD system, the lowest-resolution image (called Base/16) measures 128×192 pixels, while the highest (called Base*16) is $2,048 \times 3,072$ pixels in size, making it a high-resolution image.

HMA (IBM-compatible systems only.) High Memory Area. This term also refers to the 64K area of RAM between 1,024K and 1,088K. See **High Memory** for more information.

home page Not just for homeboys. The **Internet** is a global network of interconnected computers, and one of its most popular and growing areas is called the **World Wide Web**. The first screen that Web users encounter in searching for a particular topic is the *home page*. It's really a digital welcome mat that contains a table of contents to more information which a user will find at their **Web Site**.

HP Hewlett-Packard, a major manufacturer of computers and peripherals (scanners, printers) that was founded in 1939 by William Hewlett and David Packard.

HPGL Hewlett-Packard Graphics Language. A **vector** graphics file format developed by Hewlett-Packard for use in plotters. For more information, see **flatbed plotter**.

HSB Hue Saturation and Brightness. Based on the way that human being see color–instead of the RGB and CMYK color-producing methods typically found when working with computers and printers–this is an alternative way of looking at "real world" color. Saturation, often referred to as chroma by show-offs, is a measurement of the amount of gray present in a color. Brightness is the intensity of light present in a color. Adobe Photoshop and other image-manipulation programs allow you to control the amount of HSB in your images with individual slider controls for each element.

HTML HyperText Markup Language. A format used on **World Wide Web Home Pages** on the **Internet** that uses multimedia techniques to make the Web easy to browse.

hue An object's *hue* is based on the wavelength of light reflected from it. In plain English, it's a specific shade or tint of a particular color. *See* **HSB**.

HyperCard (Macintosh only.) A development product from Apple Computer designed for the Macintosh, to be used by "real people" for creating databases that make extensive use of graphics. HyperCard users use built-in tools to construct *stacks* of *cards* that can hold data, text, graphics, sound, and video with **HyperText** links connecting them. Apple's HyperTalk programming language allows complex applications to be developed, and third-party compilers are available that can compile stacks into stand-alone programs. While many interesting stacks were developed, HyperCard never lived up to its promise as the programming language "for the rest of us."

hypermedia A nonlinear collection of numbers, text, graphics, video, and audio as elements used in a **HyperText** system, such as the World Wide Web or a **HyperCard** stack.

HyperText A concept originally postulated by computer visionary Ted Nelson as a method for making the computer respond to the way humans think and behave. In a HyperMedia environment (like the World Wide Web), all the various forms of information including audio, video, and text are tied together—with HyperText links—so users can move from one to another by clicking software buttons with their mouse.

IBM International Business Machines. They may not have invented microcomputers, but they made the use of small computers in business more acceptable and in doing so forever changed the face of computing.

There are two major classes of small computers: Those built to the IBM standard and those that comply with the Apple Macintosh standard. IBM called its first personal computer the PC, but this term has fallen into general use to identify any computer that meets the specifications originally set by IBM. Sometimes, you will hear non-IBM PCs called *clones* although this term has fallen out of favor as companies, such as Compaq Computer, sell more PCs than IBM. More often, these computers are called IBM-compatibles or just PCs.

IBM-compatible Refers to a computer made by any manufacturer that follows the standards original set by IBM when they introduced their first personal computer. After the original standards were established, subsequent specifications–especially video standards–were driven by third-party manufacturers.

ICC The International Color Consortium is a group of eight of the largest manufacturers in the computer and digital imaging industries. The consortium works to advance cross-platform color communications, and has established base-level standards and protocols in the form of ICC Profile Format specifications, to build a common foundation for communication of color information.

ICCP The Institute for the Certification of Computer Professionals. A professional organization that does what its name says.

icon Those "little pictures" used by graphical user interfaces for operating systems such as the Macintosh or Windows 95. One new icon, by way of example, added to Windows 95 is the Recycling Bin. This is the place where you place files or documents that you want removed or erased form your hard disk. While new to Microsoft Windows, this icon, called the Trash Can, was an original icon and component of the first Macintosh operating system in 1985.

IDE Integrated Drive Electronics. The motherboard of IBM-compatibles accepts several different kinds of circuits to control the hard disks, the most common standard being IDE. Instead of connecting to a controller card, the IDE interface incorporates the drive controller functions on the drive and attaches directly to the motherboard. This standard has the advantage of being reasonably fast (7.5MB/second) and inexpensive.

IEEE The Institute of Electrical and Electronics Engineers is an organization that is actively involved in setting standards for computers and data communications. Here's an example: IEEE 1284 is a parallel port standard that is compatible with the Centronics parallel port commonly found on most PCs. This standard defines the type of cable used in order to increase distances up to 30 feet and sustain high transfer rates.

illustration program Just another name for a computer drawing program. The most popular are Adobe Illustrator and MacroMedia (formerly Aldus) FreeHand.

image editing program The broad term for software that allows digital images to be manipulated and enhanced. Typical cross-platform image editing capabilities are Adobe Photoshop and Fractal Design Painter, but are also, sometimes, called photo illustration software—to muddy the waters even further. Pixographers use image editing and manipulation software to improve and change images much as you would produce similar effects in a traditional darkroom. The advantage of working in a digital "darkroom" is that you don't have to work in the dark or get your hands wet. And more often than not, dramatic effects are easier to achieve digitally than using light-sensitive paper and photographic chemicals.

image enhancement Regardless of platform and cost, all image enhancement programs do the same thing: They manipulate the pixels of a **bitmapped** image to achieve a desired effect. You might say this is similar to a photographer working in a darkroom; he or she manipulates the silver grains in film and paper to produce a finished image. Both cases involve digital manipulation. The digital studio requires a computer, while your darkroom requires only the digits on the ends of your hands. The most popular aspect of digital photography is image editing (or enhancement). Because most image enhancement programs have the same function, many of the basic tools used are similar. Here's a quick look at some of the typical ones you can expect to find and what you can do with them:

- *Crop*: Cropping an image focuses attention on the real subject of your photograph and eliminates distractions on the edges of the frame. You can also use digital cropping tools to change the shape of the image from portrait (vertical) to landscape (horizontal) orientation.
- *Rotate*: The Rotate tool or command can also change the shape of the image from portrait to landscape orientation by simply flipping the image on end. Some image enhancement programs even have a command, tool, or menu item called *Flip*. One of the most useful applications for this tool is to rotate an image by just a degree, or fraction of a degree, to straighten horizon lines or lopsided buildings.
- *Color*: Changing an image from color to black and white or vice versa is easier digitally than using traditional techniques. Working in a wet darkroom requires using special paper, like Kodak's Panalure and dim-bulb safelights, but requires only a menu pull to accomplish digitally. If you plan to use a photograph in a black-and-white

newsletter, converting a color image to black and white makes the size of the photographic file smaller, and a smaller file takes up less on your hard disk and prints faster. Some programs allow you to colorize black-and-white photographs, and like the video process, the results can be quietly beautiful or grating, depending on your taste and creativity. You can also use colorization techniques to add brown or sepia tones to create an old-time look.

- *Brightness and Contrast*: Reducing or increasing the photograph's contrast or brightness so the output looks better than the original. This is significantly easier to do digitally than using variable contrast paper in a traditional darkroom. This can be an important tool for the digital imager. It's been my experience that most Kodak Photo CD scans can always use more contrast.

- *Lighten/Darken*: You can use image enhancement tools to produce traditional photographic techniques like "burning" and "dodging" to improve a photograph's appearance. For new photographers, or those not familiar with darkroom work, *burning* is a term for selectively darkening part of an image to hide a distracting element or bring out something hidden by highlights. *Dodging* is the reverse process and selectively lightens part of an image.

- *Pixel painting*: If the original image is not in good condition, you can use image manipulation techniques to eliminate scratches, cracks, and creases on a photograph. All of these techniques can be combined to rescue old—and some not-so-old—photographs from being lost forever.

- *Sharpening*: If there is one tool totally unique to digital imaging it's sharpening. This effect is produced by increasing the contrast of adjacent pixels, and can be applied to an entire image by using sharpening filters, or selectively by using sharpening tools found in most image editing programs.

imagebase Database programs that can be used to keep track of photographs, video clips, graphics, and even sound are sometimes referred to as *imagebase* programs.

Even before Kodak unleashed its Photo CD format on unsuspecting computer users, photographers, designers, and artists needed a method for organizing their image storage. In the past this was, more often than not, accomplished by using a flat filing cabinet that nobody in the office could ever keep straight. When computers started storing pictures as data, many graphics professionals stuffed the images on their hard disks inside folders or directories, often labeled with cryptic names. The problem became not "where did I put that artwork," but "what did I call that file?" Image databases, when properly organized, can answer both questions.

It wasn't all that long ago that you couldn't find a single image database program, but nowadays you can't walk down the aisle at CompUSA or Computer City without falling over shelves stacked high with them. What's caused this avalanche of products? Part of the answer is a massive shift of designers and artists from conventional drawing board methods to digital ones. The increase in popularity of multimedia and **Photo CD** must also take some credit for this explosion of digital images.

image pac The system that Eastman Kodak uses to write photographic images onto a **Photo CD** disc. *See* **Photo CD** for details.

imagesetter A high-quality printer that creates high-resolution text and graphics and typically accepts **PostScript** input. Instead of producing output on laser printers, imagesetters are used to produce reproduction-quality pages that can delivered to a printer.

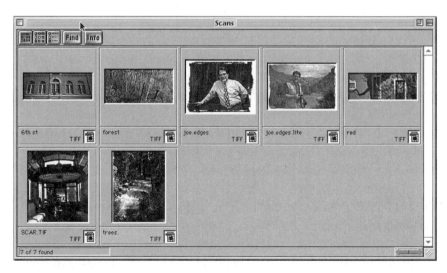

Imagebase programs, like the cross-platform Kudo Image Browser, allow users to catalog and retrieve digital photographic images. In case you're wondering, the guy with the beard in the photographs is me.

imaging Typically this terms refers to the creation of an analog image (print, negative, or transparency) from a digital photograph. If you need to make many conventional (silver-based) prints from your manipulated image, the least expensive way to make reprints is from a film original or "second original." Some service bureaus offer file-to-film imaging using the large-format-capable LVT (Light Valve Technology) film recorder. At 4,000 dpi, the LVT film recorder can produce 4×5 or 8×10 negatives or transparencies at a higher-resolution than any currently available film recorder. A service bureau or commercial lab can take an 8×10 negative produced on the LVT and print murals as large as 10×20 feet that will look as good and sharp as if they were produced from a contact inter-negative or transparency. The cost for imaging a 4×5 transparency can be $145 or more.

Paper output is one of the most traditional forms of photographic presentation. While many photographers can afford photo-realistic printers, some beginning digital pros may not be able to. Service bureaus can fill that need as well as provide output in larger sizes, up to including mural-sized images. One of the simplest services is making conventional silver prints from a negative or transparency that has been created from an original digital image. This range of service falls under the general heading of standard professional color lab services, and if your service bureau is not a professional photo lab, you can take that now-analog piece of film to any competent lab and have prints made in any size and quantity. On the other end of the spectrum is less expensive color paper output. For smaller, inexpensive prints, many service bureaus also offer output in the form of color prints from a laser copier. Output from a **dye-sublimation** printer would also be a good way to evaluate your digital experiments. It probably is not the best way to check your image for color balance, but because dye-sub prints are not that expensive, it's a good way to see how your special effects look before having costly film recorder output produced.

indexed color There are two kinds of indexed color images: those with a limited number of colors, and pseudocolor images. The number of colors for the first type is usually 256 or less. Pseudocolor images are really grayscale images that display the variations in gray levels in colors rather than shades of gray, and are typically used for scientific and technical work. CompuServe's **GIF** format creates files in indexed color. Before image-enhancement programs, like Adobe Photoshop, can use GIF files they have to be converted into **RGB** format.

infobahn Yet another term for the Information Superhighway, obviously coined by computer users who would rather be driving their Porsches instead of their Compaqs.

information superhighway Or as Kai Krause calls it, the "Super Information Highway," is a term created by pundits (although Vice-President Al Gore has been widely credited for inventing it) which refers to an interconnected telecommunications network connecting every house, business, and educational institution in the world.

INIT (Macintosh only.) Short for Initialize or Initialization. This is a small software program that is initialized (or launched) when your computer is started. INITs are loaded into your computer's RAM on startup before anything else happens. (They are displayed at the bottom of your computer screen as they are loaded.) As such, INITs can be memory hogs and Mac-heads need to be careful not to load up with so many that the operation of their computer is diminished, not having enough available memory to launch large programs like Adobe Photoshop or Microsoft Word. Currently known as Extensions, these little programs can do things as frivolous as sounds or clocks or as important as drivers for the printer that you have connected to your Macintosh.

initialize The process of setting all values on a **hard disk**, **removable media**, or **floppy disk** to *zero*; in other words, erasing all of the data that's currently there.

initialize a disk Also called *formatting* a disk. (And yes, the formatting process initializes the disk by setting all values at zero and erases all existing data.)

inkjet This kind of printer works by spraying tiny streams of quick-drying ink onto your paper and produces high-quality printing like that of a laser printer. Circuits controlled by electrical impulse or heat determine exactly how much ink—and what color—to spray to create a series of dots or lines that combine to form a printed photograph.

There are two kinds of inkjet designs: Instead of the thermal approach favored by Canon, Apple, and HP, the Epson Stylus Color family of printers uses **piezoelectric** technology that uses mechanical vibrations, instead of heat, to fire ink onto paper. Unlike its competitors, the Stylus Color places more uniform, consistent ink droplets and can deliver up to 720 dpi resolution. Unlike some color inkjet printers, the Stylus Color (except the low-end LS model) uses two ink cartridges: one for black and one for cyan, magenta, and yellow. This means if you print a lot of text or black-and-white photographs, you only have to replace the black cartridge.

input *(noun)* The information that is entered onto a computers hard disk or removable media disk is called *input*. *(verb)* Data that is entered into a computer is said to have been *input*. A photograph scanned into an image-enhancement program is *input* into it.

input device Any computer peripheral such as a **keyboard** or **scanner** that converts analog data into digital information that can be handled by your computer.

install program Sometimes called a *setup program*, it prepares the application (the shrink-wrapped program you just purchased) to run on your computer. It creates a directory or folder (sometimes several) on your hard disk and copies the files from the disks or CD-ROM disks your program was delivered with onto the computer's hard disk. In the bad old days of computing, it was up to the user to create the folders or directories and manually copy files from floppy disk onto a system's hard disk, but all programs now humanely include install programs.

Intel The leading manufacturer of microprocessor chips used in IBM-PC and compatible computers, although not the only one.

intelligent agent This latest computer buzzword refers to software that has been taught something of your desires or preferences and acts on your behalf to do things for you. The Artificial Intelligence community refers to this as *heuristic learning*. While several Intelligent Agent programs exist, none of them have scratched the surface on what is possible. Agents will be a *big* section in the next edition of this book.

integrated circuit A self-contained electronic device contained in a single semiconductor computer chip.

interface The "real world" connection between hardware, software, and the user—where the rubber meets the road. Also a mechanical or electrical link connecting two or more pieces of computer equipment. *See* **GUI**, Graphical User Interface.

interlaced Broadcast television uses an interlaced signal, and the **NTSC** standard is 525 scanning lines, which means the signal refreshes the screen every *second* line 60 times a second, and then goes back to the top of the screen and refreshes the other set of lines, again at 60 times a second. The average non-interlaced computer monitor refreshes its *entire* screen at 60 to 72 times a second, but better ones refresh the screen at higher rates. Anything over 70 **Hz** is considered flicker-free. Don't buy an interlaced monitor. You will pay in eyestrain for the few bucks you save.

interleave Refers to the way computers read and write data to and from a **hard disk**. If the computer reads or writes one sector of the hard disk, then skips one, that interleave factor is referred to as 2:1. If the controller writes one sector and then skips two, the interleave is called 3:1. The interleave factor is established by the hard disk's manufacturer. Using the correct interleave setting is critical to getting maximum performance out of your hard disk, and almost all hard disk formatting software will automatically set the proper interleave for your specific hard disk.

Internet Originally developed for military use, it is made up of thousands of interconnected computer networks in over seventy countries, connecting academic, commercial, government, and military networks for academic and commercial research. It is also used as a worldwide electronic mail system. The fastest growing part of the Internet is the **World Wide Web**, where thousands of companies are creating what might be the real **Information Superhighway**. Connection to the Internet is available through on-line services such as **CompuServe**, Prodigy, and America Online.

Internet address Fast replacing "What's your sign?" is a request for someone's Internet address. The format for addressing a message to any

Internet user is recipient@location.domain. The recipient is the person's name or "handle" (there is more than a little comparison between the hoopla surrounding the Internet and the citizen's band radio craze), the location is the place or node where the recipient can be found, and the suffix tells whether the kind of organization that the address belongs to. For example:

- EDU is educational
- ORG is organization
- COM is commercial
- GOV is government
- MIL is military

Locations outside the United States will have an additional extension identifying their country of origin.

interpolated resolution Scanners are measured by their *optical* as well their *interpolated* resolution. Optical resolution refers to the raw resolution of the scanner that's inherently produced by the hardware, while interpolated resolution is a software technique that's used to add pixels to simulate a higher resolution.

interrupt A break in a program's execution that can be caused by a signal that directs the computer to leave the software's natural sequence in such as manner that the normal flow can be resumed after the break.

I/O device Input/Output device. This is another way to refer to peripheral devices such as CD-ROM drives, printers, film recorders, etc.

IRQ An Interrupt Request line is a communication channel between any card installed in a IBM-compatible computer and the CPU.

ISA Industry Standard Architecture. This is another buzzword for the expansion slots found in PCs. Unlike older expansion slot designs, the ISA slots allow the installation of plug-in boards that can transfer data 16 bits at a time. They will also accept 8-bit cards from the original IBM-PC standard, but the speed will be limited to that of the original board's design.

ISDN Integrated Services Digital Network. A new telephone system concept that would provide an international standard for voice, data, and signaling. Because this is a purely digital system, **modems** would be replaced by simpler terminal equipment connecting computers to the telephone network. Two problems are standing in the way of widespread acceptance of ISDN: the high cost of terminal equipment and similarly high costs for telephone companies to upgrade their central office hardware and software to ISDN.

ISO International Standards Organization. Founded in 1946 with headquarters in Geneva, Switzerland, the ISO sets international standards for many fields, excluding electrical and electronics, which are controlled by the International Electrotechnical Commission (IEC). The ISO is comprised of more than 160 committees and 2,300 subcommittees and working groups, and is made up of standards organizations from more than seventy-five countries.

I-way Yet another acronym for the Information Superhighway. (Are we there yet?)

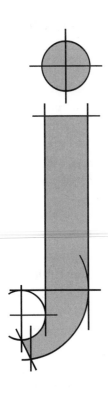

jaggies Extra pixels surrounding hard edges—especially diagonal lines—are caused by the **aliasing** features of many graphics programs. Sometimes when a graphic is displayed on a monitor, you'll see jagged edges around some objects. These rough edges are caused by an effect called aliasing. Techniques that smooth out the "jaggies" are called *anti-aliasing*.

Jaz A removable media format from Iomega Corporation that has a capacity of 1GB. (A 540MB version has also been proposed.) Unlike the **Zip** format that uses **Bernoulli box** technology, Jaz drives use a conventional **Winchester** design with 3½-inch magnetic disks. Because of the design, Jaz performance is better than Zip's. For example, a Jaz drive has a 10MB per second transfer rate, 12 ms average seek time, and 17.5 ms average access time.

joystick An input device that moves the cursor (or

game functions in games) around the screen much like a mouse would. The difference between a mouse and a joystick is the shape. A joystick has a lever that can be moved in 360 degrees and usually has buttons similar to a mouse for additional functions.

JPEG An acronym for a compressed graphics format created by the Joint Photographic Experts Group, within the International Standards Organization. Unlike other compression schemes, JPEG is what the techies call a "lossy" method. By comparison, LZW compression (*see* **GIF**) is lossless–meaning that no data is discarded during the compression process. JPEG, on the other hand, achieves compression by breaking an image into discrete blocks of pixels, which are then divided in half until a compression ratio of from 10:1 to 100:1 is achieved. The greater the compress ratio that is accomplished, the greater loss of sharpness you can expect. JPEG was designed to discard information the eye cannot normally see, but the compression process can be slow.

Julia sets A module of **Kai's Power Tools** that allows users to generate and explore using **fractals** or fractal segments for masking and mapping.

jumper A removable electrical connection found on a motherboard, along with some expansion boards and modems, that provides a change in a circuit. I've never had to move these little bits of plastic and metal on any of my Macintosh computers but have had to do so on my PC. The implementation of Microsoft Windows 95 plug-and-play standards is supposed to minimize this kind of old-fashioned, hands-on hardware manipulation.

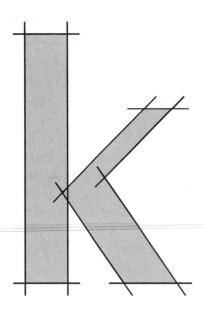

k An abbreviation for the prefix kilo or 1,000.

K In the computer world, K stands for a different type of "kilo"–in this case, 2 to the 10th power (2^{10}), or 1,024. A Kilobyte (or KB) is, therefore, not 1,000 bytes but is 1,024 bytes.

Kai's Power Tools (or KPT) A landmark series of Adobe Photoshop-compatible **plug-in filters** developed by Kai Krause for HSC Software (now called Meta-Tools). KPT, available in either the Windows or Mac versions, consists of four mini-applications and a bunch of filters. Some filters and mini-applications appear under KPT 3 in the Filters pull down menu, while other appear under the appropriate filter type in Adobe Photoshop's standard filter categories. Look at the items in the Filter menu and its submenus and you'll discover where the items contained in Kai's Power Tools are located.

Other applications included in the package are: Texture Explorer, which lets you generate texture, background, and material that can then be applied to photographs, text, backgrounds, or objects. Gradient Designer lets you mix up to 500 colors at one time, and provides sixteen combinations of mode and looping, opacity, and the ability to blend to "no color." Gradients on Paths lets you wrap any blend of colors around a free-form path or text selection. Julia Sets allows users to generate and explore using **fractals** or fractal segments for masking and mapping. These apps alone would be a good deal, but HSC also includes twenty-nine filters including Glass Lens, which lets you turn any image or part of an image into a sphere; Sharpen Intensity which goes beyond Adobe Photoshop's sharpening filter; and Hue Protected Noise.

As I write this, the folks at MetaTools began shipping the next version. Here's a sneak preview of what you might expect: KPT 3.0 will sport two new interface extensions. Spheroid Designer will create a multi-illuminated sphere with varying colored light sources, including positive and negative light. Interform will mathematically interpolate between two textures generated by Texture Explorer and provide either still or animated output. And instead of throwing KPT one-step filters all over the Filter menu, they will be grouped into user interfaces, which will (unlike the current version) allow users to create and preview effects in real time before applying. KPT 3.0 also promises to have significant speed improvements, larger preview windows, and compatibility with Adobe's video editing program, Premier. This new version will ship for Power Macintosh and Windows 95 and NT.

keyboard The major input device for computers (at least until voice commands *really* take over) using a typewriter-style layout with special keys such as **ESC**, CTRL and (on the Macintosh) COMMAND.

kHz Kilohertz or 1,000 **Hertz** (cycles per second)

killer app Every software producer's dream is the creation of a program so useful that so many people will buy it that it will ultimately drive the hardware company that produced the computer that runs it. In the Apple II days, the killer app was Visicalc (where is it today?), for the IBM-PC it was Lotus 1-2-3 (but that program has sagged somewhat from its once-lofty perch), and Aldus (now Adobe) PageMaker for the Macintosh.

kilobyte What you get when you combine 1,024 (not one thousand) bytes.

Kodak Digital Science In 1995, Kodak unveiled this brand mark to differentiate the company from other players in the competitive digital-imaging marketplace. The brand is being displayed on the company's digital imaging offerings: hardware, software, and services on a phased-in basis.

Kodak Photo CD Acquire An Adobe Photoshop-compatible **plug-in** which lets you import Photo CD images directly into the program. This makes it possible for programs that cannot normally read or import Photo CD files to do so. NIH Image, a freeware image enhancement program, reads few graphic file types but is compatible with Adobe Photoshop plug-ins. By adding Photo CD Acquire to it, the program now becomes Photo CD-aware. And while Adobe's latest version of Adobe Photoshop allows you to import a Photo CD image through its Open dialog, the methodology and steps are anything but logical. Kodak's plug-in makes it easy to find and open a Photo CD image and adds increased functionality beyond merely opening the file. The latest version provides access to the higher (sixth) resolution (4,096 × 6,144 pixels) images found on Pro Photo CD Master discs.

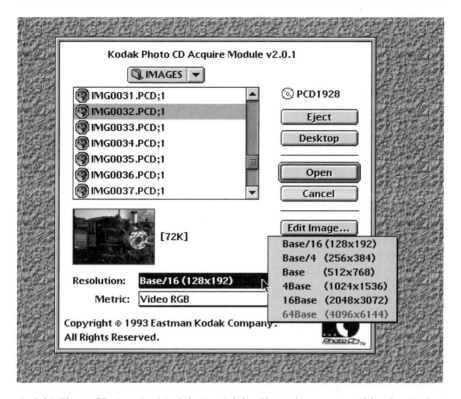

Kodak's Photo CD Acquire Module is a Adobe Photoshop-compatible plug-in that allows users of many kinds of image enhancement programs to open Photo CD images of a particular resolution and sharpen and enhance them before bringing them into the program. (Original photo © Joe Farace)

LAN Local Area Network.

landscape (mode) An image orientation that places a photograph across the wider (horizontal) side of the monitor or printer. A photographer would call this a horizontal image, but a computer user would use *landscape*. Antonym: *portrait*, or vertical. Most computer screens are horizontal, but Radius makes a monitor, called the Pivot, that uses a mercury switch that changes the orientation as the user physically rotates it from portrait to landscape.

laptop (computer) A portable computer designed to (surprise) fit on a user's lap—as opposed to a desktop model. Laptops typically have a flat screen and weigh less than ten pounds. These days, most laptops sport ports to connect an external monitor and full-size keyboard allowing them to be used as desktop models.

laser Light Amplification from the Stimulated Emission of Radiation. A device that uses precious stones, such as rubies and emeralds, to produce a precisely focused light wave and is used in communications, printing, and disk storage. While some people may think of lasers as something new, they were originally developed in 1957.

LaserJet A family of **laser printers** from **Hewlett-Packard**. The first LaserJet, introduced in 1984, made possible the desktop publishing revolution that changed, forever, how people create documents from letters to books. Up till 1994, LaserJets printed in black and white, but then HP introduced the 24-bit Color LaserJet, which was capable of printing 16.7 million colors at 300 dpi.

laser printer A printer that uses the same kind of process used by copiers to print. Inside the printer, a laser paints dots of light onto a light-sensitive drum, and toner is applied to the drum and transferred onto the paper. And like a copy machine, desktop printers use cut sheets. **IBM** introduced the first laser printer in 1975, but it wasn't until 1984 that Hewlett-Packard introduced their **LaserJet** and made desktop publishing practical for the first time.

LaserWriter A family of 300-dpi **laser printers** originally introduced by Apple Computer in 1985. All models handle bitmapped fonts, and some include **PostScript** capability.

latent image (1) In photography, this is the image that is created when a photograph is first taken–when the shutter is snapped–but the film has not yet been processed. When a roll of film is finished, but not processed, it is full of latent images.

(2) In the computer world, the definition is similar as it applies to electronic and digital image making. A latent image is an invisible image created by electrical charges. For example, in a laser printer, a latent image of the page to be copied is created on the drum before the image is transferred to the printed page that emerges as output from the printer.

launch The act of causing a program to be loaded into **RAM** and started up. This is usually done by clicking on an icon with a mouse. While originally it was Macintosh users who launched their programs this way,

PC users also speak of launching documents and programs as Microsoft Windows and Windows 95 have become more popular.

layer In image-enhancement programs, like Adobe Photoshop, layers are any one of several independent on-screen levels for creating separate—but cumulative—effects for an individual picture. Layers can be manipulated independently, and the sum of all the individual effects on each layer make up what you see as the final image.

LCD Liquid Crystal Display. A technology that uses rod-shaped crystal molecules that flow like liquid. This is the type of display typically found in **laptop** computers, but is found increasingly on sophisticated 35 mm cameras as well. In a dormant state, the crystals direct light through two polarizing filters, showing a neutral background color. When power is applied, the crystals redirect light that is absorbed in one of the polarizers, causing a dark appearance—or numbers or characters to be formed.

There are two basic types of LCD displays that are used on laptops: active and passive matrix. Passive displays appear in less-expensive laptops and provide reasonably sharp images for monochrome screens, but are much less impressive in color. One of the other negatives of passive matrix is that the cursor or pointer will occasionally disappear in a visual effect called "submarining." Many users find this annoying. Active displays are often used for color screens, but some monochrome screens, like the one in my Apple PowerBook 180 laptop, also use active matrix displays. For color applications, transistors are built into *each* pixel on the screen. A typical VGA screen requires 921,600 transistors—one for each red, green, and blue dot.

LCD printer A printer that uses a single light source directed by liquid crystal shutters instead of a laser to produce laser-like quality output and speed. There are few manufacturers of this type of printer. Qume, who makes the CrystalPrint Publisher line of printers, is one of them.

LED Light-Emitting Diode. LEDs use less power than normal incandescent light sources, but more power than LCDs.

line screen A method of reproducing continuous-tone photographs used by printers. The technique, also known as *line frequency*, is created by shooting the original photograph with a graphics art camera through a halftone screen that has many tiny dots in it. These dots are lined up in diagonal rows and the number and size of dot vary depending on the type of reproduction desired. You will often hear printers toss numbers like 80 and 133 line screen around. Here's what they mean: The lower numbers relate–inversely–to the size of the dots. The dots on a 133 screen are smaller but more numerous than on an 80 screen. Newspapers, because of the paper stock they use, often use a coarser line screen. That's why if you look closely at photographs in newspapers, you can see the dots.

Many programs, such as Adobe Photoshop, have the ability to convert your digital images into a form suitable for reproduction that will match the line screen your printer will use to print a specific document.

load This procedure occurs when a computer accepts a program or any form of data (including Photo CD images) from any kind of external storage device–a **floppy disk**, **removable media**, **CD-ROM**, etc., and store it in the computer's **RAM**.

local bus A communications path on a PC's motherboard that is located between the **CPU**, **RAM**, and expansion cards for peripheral devices that run at the speed of the CPU.

lossy compression This is exactly what is sounds like: compression techniques that do the second part of their name (compression) but do not decompress the original photograph up to 100 percent of the original image. Some images can afford small losses of resolution in order to increase compression, but that depends both on the original image and the application you have for that image. JPEG, for example, is a file format that uses a lossy compression technique.

lumen A unit of measurement used for light. A 100-watt light bulb, for example, typically generates 1,200 lumens.

luminance The amount of brightness, measured in lumens, that is given off by a pixel or area on a screen. It is the black/gray/white information in a video signal. The color model used by Kodak for its **Photo CD** process involves the translation of data originally in RGB form into what scientists call luminance and chrominance–or color and hue.

LVT Live Valve Technologies, a division of Eastman Kodak. Manu-facturers of a film recorder which produces higher-resolution output than any other film recorder (right now, anyway) and can produce up to 8×10 transparencies and negatives. A **service bureau** lab can take the 8×10 negatives produced on an LVT film recorder and print murals as large as 10×20 *feet* that look as sharp as they would have if produced from an internegative or transparency.

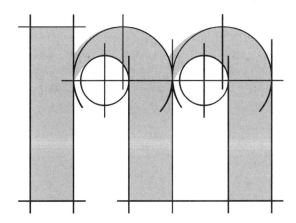

M, MB, mega One million.

Macintosh Apple Computer's personal computer that was the first *popular* computer–the ill-fated Xerox Star was probably the first–to use a graphical user interface and mouse pointing device. There are two general classes of small computers: those built to the IBM standard and those that comply with the Apple Macintosh standard. In 1995 the first Macintosh clones were built by several companies that have licensed Apple's technology. They are forbidden by their licenses to call these computers "Macintosh," so it will be interesting to hear what term gets accepted as Mac-compatible.

macro The shortened version of *macro instruction*. A macro is a short series of commands that can be programmed to perform a series of actions when triggered by a simple keystroke or keystroke combination. Many programs, like Microsoft Word or Excel, allow users–

who are non-programmers—to create macros to help them accomplish repetitive tasks.

Magic Wand The Magic Wand, a powerful selection tool found in Adobe Photoshop and other image-enhancement programs, selects not on the basis of shape but on similarity of color. When you click on an individual pixel in an image, the Magic Wand selects pixels that have the same color plus similar shades of that color. How many similarly colored shades are selected depends on the *Tolerance* specified in the Magic Wand's palette. The smallest Tolerance value you can enter is zero and the largest is 255. The **default** is 32, and a little trial and error helps you refine the number you will want to set for a given photograph. Keep in mind that Tolerances will vary based on the image. A good rule of thumb is that when selecting a predominantly solid color, lower tolerances work best. But be careful. If you set Tolerances too large, you will select areas you don't want. To assist with the selection process, Adobe Photoshop's Select menu offers additional commands that increase the efficiency of whatever tool you may be using. The Grow command, for example, temporarily doubles the Tolerance range for the Magic Wand. Another way to increase the selection being made is to use the Similar command. When you do the selection can jump over areas to find other colors that fit within the specified Tolerance.

In Fractal Design's Painter, you will notice that the Magic Wand does not appear as a tool, but instead is found as a command. Unlike most image-enhancement programs' implementation of this tool, Painter doesn't contain a **dialog box** that allows you to select a range of pixels. Instead, you simply select the menu command and click and drag the cursor across the part of the image that you want to select. When you do, the selected area is overlaid with a red **mask**. To select more areas, hold the Shift key and drag the wand across another area. Pretty neat, huh?

magnetic bubble A method that uses magnetic film for storing information as a pattern of magnetic fields. Magnetic bubble devices are non-volatile and hold data even when power is lost.

magneto-optical This class of removable drives uses the ability of lasers to heat material and thus change reflectivity to produce media that can be erased and reused. One of the negatives of optical drives is that writing data to optical media requires three spins. The first erases existing data, the second writes new data, and the third verifies the data is there. When compared to magnetic drives, all this spinning tends to reduce performance. Typical performance specifications for magneto-optical drives (e.g., Fujitsu 230MB unit) are seek times of 30 ms, access time of 40 ms and average write transfer rate of .44 per second. The drives are more expensive than magnetic drives—although the media is less so, and like their magnetic competitors, manufacturers have yet to standardize a single magneto optical format.

MASER Microwave Amplification by Stimulated Emission of Radiation.

mask Many image enhancement programs have the ability to create masks—or stencils—that are placed over the original image to protect parts of it and allow other sections to be edited or enhanced. Cutouts or openings in the mask make the unmasked portions of the image accessible for manipulation while the mask protects the rest. Graphic artists who previously used Rubylith material to create masks will be glad to find that digital masks are part of their repertoire too.

mass storage Any computer storage device capable of handling large amounts of data. What defines "large" is a sliding scale. Currently 2 or more gigabyte drives are considered *large*, but I remember a time when I installed a 105MB drive in my Mac IIci and someone in the industry asked me "What do you need all that space for? You'll never fill it up." Today a 500MB hard disk is considered the rock bottom minimum for any kind of graphics application.

Maximize In Microsoft Windows, the Maximize button appears as an "up-arrow" button at the far right of a title bar in a window. Clicking the button enlarges the window to full size. While the form of the button has changed somewhat with Windows 95, the function is identical.

MCA Micro Channel Architecture. A bus or slot arrangement found only on some IBM-brand PS/2 machines and in few others. Micro Channel transfers data at 20MB/sec, and has modes for increasing speeds to 40 and 80MB and has specifications that allow for 64 bits and 160MB transfer. MCA boards are not interchangeable with ISA and EISA boards.

This standard was touted by IBM as the next big thing in bus design, but not many manufacturers were as enamored of it as IBM was.

megabyte What you have when you lasso 1,024 Kilobytes. Often called just "meg" and abbreviated **MB**.

menu bar In any graphical user interface (such as Macintosh or Windows), the menu bar is that portion of a window at its top that contains a row of onscreen menus.

Metafile This multifunction graphic file type accommodates both vector and bitmapped data within the same file. While seemingly more popular in the Windows environment, Apple's **PICT** format is a metafile.

MHz MegaHertz or 1,000,000 cycles per second.

MICR Magnetic Ink Character Recognition is the type of font and ink type used on checks so they can be read by computers.

microcomputer A complete small computer system that includes a keyboard, monitor, memory (RAM), and microprocessor (CPU).

Microsoft An industry powerhouse that developed the **MS-DOS** operating system and Windows **GUI**, the software that runs over 80 percent of the microcomputers in the world. In 1975, Microsoft was founded by Paul Allen and Bill Gates, who wrote the first BASIC language interpreter for the Intel 8080 microprocessor that powered the first IBM-PC. Microsoft is also extremely successful in the production of applications. Its Excel spreadsheet for the Macintosh has been so successful that it has driven out all its competitors and is now the de facto standard. Interestingly, Microsoft does not offer any graphics or image-enhancement programs other than its presentations-oriented PowerPoint.

MIDI A student at the Naval Academy in Annapolis, Maryland. NOT! Although pronounced "middie," it stands for Musical Instrument Digital Interface, a standard that describes how computers and MIDI-compatible musical increments interface. MIDI is hardware that includes plugs and connectors that connect musical instruments to your computer or sound board. MIDI is also a set of rules for how music should be encoded so that the instruments and computers can communicate.

mini-disc A 2½-inch compact disc format that can both record and play seventy-four minutes of sound. Currently it is only used for consumer music applications similar to portable cassette and CD players, but Sony has been pushing the device for use in computers much the same way music CDs drove the implementation of CD-ROM devices. Right now the only thing standing in the way of wider acceptance of the mini-disc is the cost. But if history is any indication, this may be short-lived. Watch for mini-discs in future computers.

Minimize In Microsoft Windows, the Minimize button appears as a down-arrow button at the immediate right of a title bar. Clicking the Minimize button shrinks a window to its icon. While the form of the button has changed somewhat with Windows 95, the function is identical.

MIPS Million Instructions Per Second. MIPS has always been a measure of computer performance by indicating how fast a CPU can process software instructions. To give you some idea how much real computing power is available in today's desktop computers, in the disco seventies, MIPS cost $800,000, which dropped to $250,000 by the eighties. In 1991 the cost of MIPS had dropped to $93 and by the beginning of 1996 cost only $20!

modem The strict definition is *mo*dulate-*dem*odulate. Since the current telephone system across most of America is analog, computer data must be converted from digital form into analog form for transmission over telephone lines. At the other end, the data is then converted from analog back into digital form. A modem, when used with the appropriate software, can also dial a call to an on-line service or **BBS**, answer a call, and control transmission speed, which currently ranges from 300 to 28,800 bps (bits per second.) While modem speeds have continuously been raised through a horsepower race between manufacturers, all this conversion back and forth ultimately limits the ultimate speed of data communications. The **ISDN** system is an all-digital one that would eliminate modems as we know them, in favor of terminals at each end. Whether ISDN catches on depends on the success of the cable TV industry's entry (as well as satellite program suppliers, like SBSS) into the data delivery business.

monitor Another word for the box containing the screen, its power supply, and other components that enable you to see a digital image displayed. That's why you often hear some monitors called "displays." Because monitors look so much like television sets, many computer users get confused when shopping for a monitor. For instance, when you trade-in your 19-inch TV set for a 30-inch Sony, you expect to see the same image you saw on your old TV—except bigger. This doesn't happen with monitors. In addition to a larger screen, greater resolution is possible. This enables you to see *more* of the same image. A 15-inch monitor, for example, can display a 800×600 pixel image, while a 19-inch model will let you see $1,280 \times 1,024$ pixels.

A word about screen size: Manufacturers have routinely overstated the screen sizes of monitors in much the same way that TV set builders have historically done. A 17-inch monitor has an actual viewing area of 15.8 inches, providing 18.89 square inches less of usable screen area—a 13% reduction. Recently, a lawsuit challenging this long-standing industry practice was settled by companies including Apple Computer, Compaq, Dell Computer, IBM, Nanao USA, NEC, Samsung, and ViewSonic. Terms of the contract state that all monitors built after February 1, 1996 must be described by their actual viewable area. The settlement states: "Defendants cannot refer to the computer display as 15 inches unless the viewable area is also disclosed."

Other than screen size and resolution, the next most important factors in evaluating your choice of monitors is **dot-pitch**, **refresh rate**, and whether the monitor is **multiscan** or **interlaced**.

monitor setup When starting to work with digital images, photo-graphers automatically assume that what they see on their screen will be what the 4×5 transparency that comes back from their service bureau will look like. They think that the color balance and density (lightness/darkness) of the image on their monitor will match the service bureau's output. Unfortunately, that is not always so. That's one of the reasons that image enhancement programs, like Adobe Photoshop, include a feature like Monitor Setup to let you adjust the parameters in your computer's monitor. Adobe Photoshop's Monitor Setup dialog box contains built-in

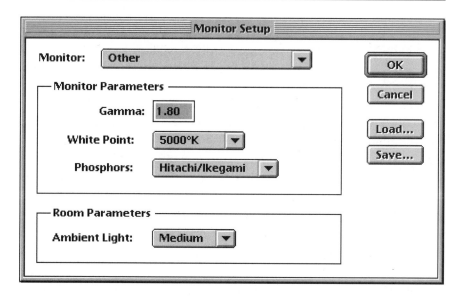

Adobe Photoshop's Monitor Setup dialog box allows Macintosh and Windows users to "set up" their monitors so that what they see on the screen more closely approximates the output—whether it be from a printer or film recorder. While not specifically a method of color matching, Monitor Setup is the first step in making sure that what you see onscreen is what you get for a result.

settings for thirty off-the-shelf monitors. You won't have any problems if you have one of these thirty, but what if your monitor isn't listed? You'll need to go on to the next step.

The first one is *Gamma*, which represents the brightness of the medium colors displayed on the screen. If you have a light screen, the Gamma level will be below 1.0. If the screen is inherently dark, a value greater than 3.0 will be required. Tweaking Gamma for non-listed monitors is expedited by the Gamma Control Panel that Adobe includes with Adobe Photoshop. This easy-to-use utility lets you adjust the red, blue, and green intensities of your individual monitor.

The next part is *White Point*, which represents the **color temperature** of the lightest color your screen can produce. I keep mine set at 6,500 degrees Kelvin, but well-heeled purists can check their monitor with Minolta's CRT Color Analyzer. Price tag: $10,000.

The five options in the *Phosphors* menu fit most computer monitors, including video projectors like the Barco. The custom option lets you select RGB levels for both the X and Y coordinates of the screen. This is not intended for mere mortals, but technical support from the company that made your particular monitor should be able to supply that information along with the correct White Point.

Lastly, Adobe Photoshop lets you adjust your monitor for room conditions ranging from dark to light. I keep mine set on "medium" and I have so much ambient light from two large windows in my office that I can turn off the room lights and can work comfortably.

monochrome A monochrome monitor displays one color on a different colored background. In the Macintosh environment this means a black-and-white screen, while in the PC world it can also be amber or green on a black background.

morph Morphing (short for Metamorphosis) is a graphics technique that blends two different shapes over a short period of time. A sequence might start with an image of a view camera and over time the camera in Kafka-like fashion gradually metamorphosizes into, say, a computer. In other words, the camera was "morphed" into the computer. Before "morph" became such a hot buzzword, some graphics software called this technique "Tweening" because it changes an object's shape *between* one end of a sequence and another.

MOS Metal Oxide Semiconductor.

motherboard A plastic board containing printed circuitry and chips that when working together make "the machine go ping." The motherboard holds the **RAM**, device controllers (e.g., **CD-ROM**, **hard drive**, tape backup mechanism), the **bus**, and the main processing chip called the **CPU**, or Central Processing Unit, although there are some computer users that call the entire box a **CPU**. In the Apple Macintosh environment you will often hear the motherboard called **logic board**, while the term "motherboard" remains more popular with PC users. Occasionally you will see a product called a "daughterboard." This kind of circuit board attaches (plugs into) other cards installed in the computer or the motherboard itself.

Technology Update: A recent report on CNN about a company called The Panda Project may sound the death knell for motherboard technology as we know it. Panda is the creation of Stanford Crane and Joseph Sarubbi, the inventor of the original IBM-PC. Panda recently introduced its series of two motherboardless computers called the Archistat, which uses high-density connectors that Panda created to treat CPUs and other components as Lego blocks used to assemble the system *du jour*. A Panda box can be a Mac one day, a PC the next—or even later on the same day. What effect the motherboardless technology will have on tomorrow computer systems is unknown, but we'll give you an update in the next edition.

mouse An integral part of any graphical user interface is the ability to use a pointing device. The most common is called a *mouse* because of its oval shape and the tail-like cable that connects it to the keyboard (Mac) or back of the computer (PC). When using a mouse, movement is relative; as you move the mouse, the screen pointer moves in relation to it. Mice come in many forms, including a tailless, wireless model along with optical and mechanical ones. The wire, mechanical variety is the most popular. **Graphics tablets** which use a pen-like stylus and motion-sensitive drawing pads to create freehand drawings are cousins of the mouse.

MPEG Moving Pictures Experts Group. Does for digital video what **JPEG** does for digital still images. This is an ISO standard for compressing full-motion video and it provides more compression than JPEG because it takes advantage of the fact that full-motion video is made up of successive frames that consist of areas which do not change. MPEG I provides a resolution of 320×240 pixels at 30 frames per second with 24-bit color and digital audio. MPEG I is used in CD-ROMs and Video CDs, while MPEG II is a broadcast-quality video standard.

MS-DOS Microsoft Disk Operating System. Before there was Windows, MS-DOS, or DOS for short, was the name of the game for users of IBM-compatible machines. (The IBM-labeled version was called PC-DOS.) DOS features a command-line interface that enables users to interact with their computers by typed commands. To format or erase a disk you need to type FORMAT A:. If you use a semicolon instead of the colon, you get an error message. If you leave off the colon, you get another error message. The precise nature of the commands required by DOS endeared it to some people, but made the microcomputer difficult to use for others. Microsoft's original version of Windows attempted to make computers easier to use and made PCs easier to use but at the same time, slower. That's because Windows in an "environment" that requires MS-DOS to work. (That's what slows it down.) A Windows screen is divided into, well, windows that contain separate information. Theoretically, Microsoft's Windows 95 does not require DOS but it still provides access to the former command-line interface.

MTBF Mean Time Between Failure. A measurement by which hardware is expected to perform for a specified number of hours without failing. Often hard and removable drive companies will supply this information as part of their specifications. For computer users who spend more than four hours a day at their computers, MTBF is a good tool for comparing products. For light users, it may be less important.

MTTR Mean Time to Repair.

multi-format drives Something new in removable media drives, these are devices that read more than a single type of media. The first of this new breed is Panasonic's PowerDrive2. In addition to being a quad-speed CD-ROM drive, the PowerDrive2 can also read and write to 650MB optical cartridges. With a list price under $1,000, the drive is SCSI-based and works on both Mac and Windows platforms. The only negative I can see is that the drive uses a proprietary optical cartridge, but being able to back up or write to 650MB of data might make it bearable.

multiplex The ability to transmit two or more signals on a data transmission system.

multiscan MultiSync is a trademark of NEC, but many people use that term when describing any multiscan monitor. On a typical monitor, a scanning beam starts at one corner and traces a single, pixel-wide, horizontal line, then goes on to trace the next line. How fast the monitor does both horizontal and vertical scans varies depending on the kind of graphics card used. A multiscan monitor is one that automatically matches the signal sent to it by the graphics card (or Apple motherboard). If you don't have a multiscan monitor, it's important that your graphics card match the scan rate of your monitor. A multiscan monitor does all the work making sure board and monitor match. This inconsistency of scan rates is common in the PC world, but not with the Macintosh. Nevertheless, multiscan monitors work well with a Mac.

Multisync A trademark of NEC Technologies for *multiscan*.

multi-tasking Often written *multitasking*, but I find it easier to read with the hyphen. The ability of the computer's operating system to allow for two or more operations to be performed simultaneously. For example, while typing this line, I can be listening to a Bruce Cockburn music CD on my **CD-ROM** drive using Apple's CD Audio Player software, and downloading a file from CompuServe using CompuServe Information Manager software. While both Macintosh and Windows have offered some form of multi-tasking, purists scoff at both platforms' ability to offer the kind of capabilities found in mainframe operation, but regular users are more than happy being able to do what I mention in my example.

multi-user A system—or software—that can be used by two or more users at the same time.

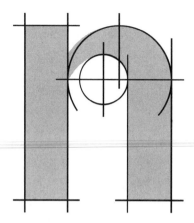

NACOMEX National Computer Exchange is an organization that tracks and publishes the street prices of used PCs. Like the so called "blue book" used by car dealers, there are price guides available to help the used-computer shopper find out what specific *used* computers models cost. Magazines, like *ComputerUSER*, prints the National Computer Exchanges' used computer prices in the back of each issue. You'll also find used Macintosh listings from the American Computer Exchange (AMCOMEX) in publications like *MacWorld*. You can safely use these prices as a guide to what you should pay for the used computer of your choice.

nano- I hate to disappoint any readers who may be *Mork & Mindy* fans, but nano is a prefix that means one-billionth.

narrow bandwidth A communication channel that can only transmit at slow speeds. The opposite is **wide**

bandwidth channels, that can transmit data–including images, sounds, and video–at high speeds.

National Bureau of Standards The NBS, located in Gaithersburg, Maryland, is the official government organization that prepares non-Department of Defense communications standards. They also operate a testing service to ensure products' conformity to standards.

native mode This is the normal mode of a computer when executing programs, as compared to **emulation** mode. This is also the highest performance level for a 486 or Pentium computer when running in Protected Mode. When Apple Computer introduced its Power Macintosh series of computers, which used RISC-base PowerPC chips, only programs written to take advantage of the chip's native mode benefitted from the additional performance available from the PowerPC. In order to run older programs, Power Macintoshes run in emulation–not native mode–which decreases performance, but makes the machine compatible with new and existing programs. For software to run at the higher speeds the new machines are capable of, applications have to be rewritten to run in native mode. When you see a sticker on a software package that says "Accelerated for Power Macintosh," it has been re-written in native mode.

netiquette When corresponding via **e-mail** and messages posted on **BBS**, on-line services, or the Internet, certain levels of civilized behavior are expected. Instead of Emily Post, the people reading your posting will show you the proper forms of written behavior. One of the most common mistakes many newcomers make is typing everything in CAPITAL LETTERS. This is considered a breach of netiquette because the writer is considered to be shouting–and it's also hard to read, too. If you get loud or profane, expect a stern warning from the **Sysop**, or you may even be barred from the forum or BBS.

network A group of computers that are interconnected by hardware and software, as in Local Area Networks or **LAN**.

Newton Apple Computer's Personal Data Assistant (PDA) a hand-held device combining the function of a computer with a Day Timer featuring input by hand-writing with a stylus that (mostly) works. Apple's Newtons are now called MessagePads, and Motorola offers a similar model called Envoy.

NeXT A company formed by Apple co-founder Steven Jobs in 1985. The company created a family of high-resolution, UNIX-based computers in 1988, but it never achieved the prominence or acceptance of the Macintosh. Manufacturing stopped in 1993, and Japan's Canon, a company investor, took over rights to the hardware design. Ross Perot, another investor, also pulled out. As I write this, NeXT is an asterisk in the history of the personal computer.

NIH (1) Not Invented Here. An attitude all too prevalent in modern corporations and organizations.

(2) National Institute of Health, *see* **NIH Image**.

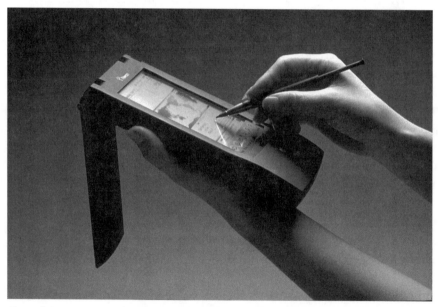

One of the most popular Personal Data Assistants, Apple's Newton MessagePad, combines low-level computer functions with a personal organizer tied together with an interface featuring handwritten input. While originally criticized for its lackluster performance, improvements in the Newton's software has made it into a useful tool, and now PDAs are also available from Motorola and Sony.

NIH Image A freeware image-enhancement program originally developed as a scientific and technical imaging tool by the National Institute of Health—as a taxpayer, you've already paid for it. It has evolved to the point where the program has many features the experimental-minded, Mac-using digital imager may appreciate. The program can acquire, display, edit, enhance, analyze, print, and even animate images. NIH Image can perform image-processing functions, such as contrast enhancement, density profiling, smoothing, and sharpening and can draw lines, rectangles, ovals, and text. It will also let you flip, rotate, invert, and scale selections.

NIH Image doesn't read many different types of graphics file formats. As it stands, Image will only read uncompressed TIFF files—although it will import Text and MCID (files compatible with the IBM-PC based MCID image-analysis system from Imaging Research). Image does, however, support Adobe Photoshop compatible plug-ins, including filters and Acquire plug-ins like Kodak's Photo CD. Installing this add-on makes acquiring Photo CD images with Image just as easy as using any other image-enhancement program.

There are currently three versions of Image: One's been designed for Macintoshes that have math coprocessors, one for the Power Macintosh (the latest version), and the third is for computers, such as the LC and Color Classic, which don't have a math coprocessor chip. Here's how to tell the difference: The math coprocessor version is marked **FPU** for "floating point unit." What makes Image especially interesting is that it is a *free* image-enhancement program that can be found on most on-line services, like CompuServe or America Online and user groups or services that sell disks of shareware or freeware.

node (1) In communications, a *node* is a point connecting a terminal or computer. You will also hear local telephone numbers that allow modem equipped computer users to connect to on-line services such as CompuServe, America Online, and Prodigy referred to as *nodes*.

(2) In computer graphics, an end point of a graphical element, a line or curve.

(3) In database management, an item of data that can be accessed by two or more routes.

Nom de Plume (Macintosh only.) If you find that creating an **alias** can be more trouble than it's worth, you need a freeware Control Panel called Nom de Plume. It's the fastest, easiest way to create aliases I've found. Author Bill Monk created this Control Panel when he got disgusted with what he calls the "Alias Two-Step." You have to dig through your Applications folder, select something, make the alias, shuffle some folders, throw the alias into the Apple Menu Items folder, pull down the Apple menu, notice that it's now about a mile wide, open the Apple Menu Items folder, and edit out the word "alias" to make it shorter. All this while waiting for the I-beam to appear in the System 7 Finder.

Nom de Plume's dialog box, which resembles the standard Open dialog, lets you simultaneously select the item you want an alias created from, name it, then place it wherever you want. If you need to create a new folder, the dialog lets you do that too. Using Nom de Plume is so seamless it makes you wonder why Apple didn't make it a part of the system software. This utility is freeware, but making copies for commercial purposes is prohibited. Nom de Plume is available exclusively through Ziff Communications on-line services and electronic publishing projects, and the author requests that it not be posted on other services.

notebook (computer) Any laptop computer that weighs from five to seven pounds is called a *notebook*. If it weighs under five pounds, it is usually called a *subnotebook*.

NTSC National Television Standards Committee. NTSC sets the standards that apply to television and video playback on resolution, speed, and color. All television sets in the United States (and Japan too, as it turns out) follow the NTSC standard as do videotape and other forms of video display, like games.

NuBus A 32-bit bus (slot) architecture originally developed at MIT and adapted by Apple Computer to use in their Macintosh II series of computers and every model since them. Many Macs have one or more NuBus slots for expansion, but all new Power Macintosh computers have adopted the PC-style PCI slots design. For all intents, the NuBus design is a dead one, although rumors persist that Apple will be building new Macs with both NuBus and PCI slots. I don't believe it.

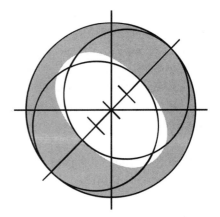

object-oriented graphics *See* **Vector.**

OCR Optical Character Recognition. This is a technique used by scanning software to convert scanned text documents into a form that can be edited with a word processor. Unless the scanner is easy to use, regardless of how high its resolution may be, you will not be able to get usable results. This is especially important if you plan on using your scanner for optical character recognition. When shopping for scanners, my recommendation is that you base 60 percent of your decision on software and the rest on hardware specifications.

A word of advice about using *hand scanners* for OCR: Some hand scanner manufactures bundle OCR software, such as OmniPage Direct AnyFont, that can (ostensibly) convert scanned text into digital documents. OCR with hand-held scanners can be tricky and your success converting scans into documents will depend on how steady and straight your scans are.

offline Anything not under the direct control of the **CPU** is said to be offline. The opposite is **online**.

one-off A **CD-ROM** disc that is made *one at a time* instead of being stamped from a glass master disc the way that discs are usually made in volume. When a new CD-ROM disc is in production, a test disc or one-off will be created for approval purposes. CD-ROM recorders are commonly called one-off machines because they write a single disc, one at a time.

online Anything under the direct control of the **CPU** is said to be online. The opposite is **offline**.

on-line services On-line services are sometimes called on-line databases, erroneously so, because they're more than that. An on-line service is an electronic source—a supermarket may be a good analogy—that lets you research an encyclopedia, the content of newspapers and magazine, as well as make and check airline reservations, send and receive e-mail (electronic mail), get answers to questions, and much, much more. One of the largest online services is **CompuServe**, whose full name is Compu-Serve Information Services and is sometimes abbreviated CIS. It's a service you can access with your modem, but you'll need software to use it effectively.

operating system Often abbreviated OS, the operating system is the master software that controls the computer. When you turn on any computer, the OS is the first thing that gets loaded into the computer's memory. The OS interacts with your computer's **ROM** (Read-Only Memory) and **BIOS** (Basic Input Output System) chips to accomplish tasks like controlling the hardware components of your system and how they interact with you through onscreen communications. The most common operating systems are the Macintosh OS, **MS-DOS** (Microsoft Disk Operating System), OS/2 (IBM's Operating System/2), and **UNIX**, with Mac and Windows leading the pack.

optical drives Optical **removable media** drives are more properly called *magneto-optical drives*, and use a laser to heat and thus change disc reflectivity to produce media that can be erased and reused. Writing data

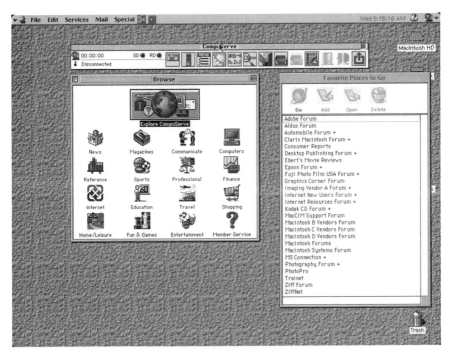

On-line services, like CompuServe, provide cross-platform software—such as the CompuServe Information Manager (for Macintosh) shown here—that makes connecting and browsing around a matter of pointing and clicking.

to optical media requires three spins: The first erases existing data, the second writes the data, and the third verifies the data is there. When compared to the operation of magnetic media drives, all of this spinning tends to reduce performance. Typical performance specifications for magneto-optical drives (based on the Fujitsu 230MB unit) are a seek time of 30 ms, access time of 40 ms and average write transfer rate of .44MB per second. On top of that, the drives are more expensive than magnetic drives—although the media is less so. And like their magnetic competitors, manufacturers have yet to standardize on a single optical format.

For savings that cost-justify systems, any practical optical media drive must fill the following needs:

1. Productivity gains measured by increased **throughput**, short cycle times, and reduced cost.
2. Information protection whose longevity and archivability are measured by standards compliance.

3. Assured information availability, or plain old **uptime**, measured by cycles without error (**MTBF**) and time to restore operation (**MTTR**).
4. Ease of integration into your operation. This can be measured by the extent of impact on current systems, schedules, and system expansion plans.
5. Volumetrics. The media capacity when measured by cost per storage unit.

optical resolution Scanners are measured by their *optical* as well and an *interpolated* resolution. Optical resolution refers is the raw resolution of the scanner that's inherently produced by the hardware, while interpolated resolution is a software technique that's used to add pixels to simulate a higher resolution. How well your scanner does this depends on the software, but in general, the average user will be pleased with the results. Purists, however, will ignore the interpolated resolution specifications and base their purchasing decision on the stated optical resolution only.

orange book *See* **CD-ROM**.

OS *See* **Operating System**.

OS/2 A single-user operating system developed by IBM that runs DOS and Windows as well as OS/2-specific apps. It provides a graphical user interface (like Windows and the Mac) as well as a command-line structure such as found in MS-DOS and many OS/2 and DOS commands are identical. OS/2 is a multi-tasking operating system, which means users can keep more than one program active at the same time.

OS/2 Warp Trying to cash in on many computer users' infatuation with *Star Trek*, IBM called OS/2 3.0, OS/2 Warp. It is an enhanced version of the original operating system that's designed to run on computers that have 4MB of RAM. OS/2 Warp includes multimedia support, **Internet** capabilities, and IBM Works.

output The analog form of information produced or generated by a computer. While historically this has referred data printed on some form of paper, it now means any kind of "real world" translation of data, including photographs, overhead transparencies, slides, or negatives.

For some reason, image output is one of the least talked-about of the elements that make up the final aspect of the digital imaging process. Output can take many different forms. An image can simply be viewed and cataloged on a monitor. Photographs can be transferred to other computers in digital form floppy disk or by any kind of removable media drive–like Iomega's Jaz or optical media–and viewed on another computer. A printer attached to your computer can produce a grayscale or color page.

In the past the selection of photo-realistic printers was limited and expensive, but all that has changed. Now you can use the growing number of inexpensive color printers from Apple and Epson to print images directly from your computer. The quality of this output is far from photographic, but it isn't bad, considering the cost. More expensive, photo-quality output is available from dye-sublimation printers, but the printers themselves and the consumables get expensive. One approach that straddles both alternatives is to output image to a color laser copier, such as Canon's. This service is available from many **service bureaus** and, depending of the quantity of prints you need, can be cost-effective. The image can be converted back into a silver-based form. Larger service bureaus and professional labs have equipment that can take your enhanced digital image and output it as a slide or 4×5 and 8×10 sheet film. Once back into silver-based form, you can use this image to project or make prints in the traditional manner.

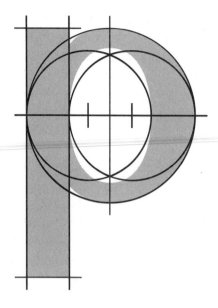

PAL Phase Alternating Line. A European video standard similar to the **NTSC** standard used by the United States and Japan. The PAL standard has a broadcast resolution of 625 lines at twenty-five interlaced frames per second. VHS tapes recorded in the PAL standard are not playable on a VHS set up for the NTSC standard and vice-versa.

palette On graphics and photo-enhancement software, a palette is a grouping of graphics tools (e.g., selection, Paint Brush, **Magic Wand**, etc.) indicated by a series or row of icons. Mouse-clicking one of the icons activates the tool and often brings up a small dialog box that contains specific options for that tool.

parallel interface A type of port found on PCs used for connecting printers, modems, and other peripheral devices. The parallel reference means that data—several bits at a time—is simultaneously sent and received over individual but adjacent wires. Some dye-sublimation printers, like the Fargo Pictura 310, require a parallel connection (because it's faster when handling large amounts of data) and provide **NuBus** interface cards for the Macintosh, which has no parallel interface ports.

PARC Palo Alto Research Center. Xerox Corporation's research and development center where the original graphical user interface and mouse interface were developed.

parity The technique of adding an extra **bit** to a block of bits in data transmission used to verify accuracy. The extra bit is called a *parity bit*.

partition This term, more common in the PC environment, is used to describe parts of the **hard disk** that are divided into several individual sections which the computer treats as separate hard disks. Each section is called a *partition* and the act of creating these sections is called *partitioning*.

patch A (usually) small program that modifies an application to repair bugs or conflicts with other software. For example, here's an excerpt from the READ ME file for Connectix RAM Doubler 1.6 patch: "Power Macintosh/Performa 5200/6200 series compatibility is implemented. Transferring a file to a floppy in DOS mode on the 6100 DOS Compatible now works. AppleMail enclosures with PowerTalk now transfer correctly. File transfer over certain LocalTalk configurations now completes." When the little patch program is run, it updates my existing copy of Ram Doubler to version 1.6, which includes the above fixes and other enhancements. Such patches are usually made available, at no cost, to registered owners of programs on on-line services, like CompuServe or America Online.

PC The generic term for Personal Computer, although originally trade-marked by IBM to describe its first personal computer. There are two major classes of personal computers: those built to the IBM standard and those that comply with the Apple Macintosh standard. IBM called its first personal computer the PC, but this term has fallen into general use to identify any computer that meets the specifications originally set by IBM. Sometimes, you will hear non-IBM PCs called **clones**, although this term has taken on a pejorative connotation as companies, such as Compaq

Computer, sell more PCs than IBM. More often, these computers are called IBM-compatibles or just PCs. In 1995, the first Macintosh clones were built by several companies that licensed Apple's technology. They are forbidden by their licenses to call these computers "Macintosh," so it will be interesting to hear what term gets accepted for "Mac-compatible."

PC card The latest, hot-from-the-oven replacement buzzword for the (mouthful) **PCMCIA**. Equipment manufacturers, such as **SyQuest**, who introduced the SQ1100 PC Card that contains a 2-inch removable media cartridge capable of storing 100MB of data.

PCD This is an **extension** used in the IBM-PC environment to describe Kodak's **Photo CD** graphics file format. PC users also use .PCD as a file extension for Photo CD image files.

PC-DOS Personal Computer Disk Operating System. This is IBM's version of **MS-DOS** and for all practical purposes is completely identical.

PCI local bus Personal Computer Interconnect is the faster successor to the VL bus and often will sit alongside an ISA slot on a motherboard. Until recently, PCI slots were limited to IBM-compatible machines. In their next generation of Power Macintosh computers, Apple Computer is abandoning their proprietary NuBus slot architecture in favor of the PCI bus. If you can't beat 'em, join 'em.

PCL Printer Control Language was first used by Hewlett-Packard Laser-Jet **printers**, but has become a standard used by many printers and **imagesetters**.

PCM (For techies only.) Pulse Code Modulation.

PCMCIA Acronym for *Personal Computer Memory Card International Association*. The cards referred to in the organization's title are small credit-card sized modules that were originally designed to plug into standardized sockets of laptop and notebook-sized computers.

To date, there have been three PCMCIA standards: Type I, Type II, and Type III. The major differences between the types is the thinness of the cards. Type III are 10.5 mm thick. Type II is 5 mm thick, and Type I is

3.5 mm thick. The modules come in many applications that vary depending on the type and thickness. For example, there are PCMCIA cards for additional memory, **hard disks**, **modems**–name it. PCMCIA cards are quickly becoming the de facto method for storing images for digital camera. Even inexpensive cameras, like Kodak's DC50, use removable PCMCIA cards to supplement the camera's built-in image storage capacity.

PCMCIA has become such a mouthful to say that at COMDEX 95, manufacturers of these wonderful devices have agreed on a new buzzword to replace it. If you see the term *PC Card*, what they really mean is PCMCIA.

PCX Not an acronym (it doesn't stand for anything specific); a bitmapped file format originally developed for the popular program PC Paintbrush. Most popular Windows and DOS graphics programs read and write PCX files.

PDA Personal Data Assistant. *See* **Newton**.

PDF The Adobe Portable Document Format is a cross-platform file format created by Adobe's Acrobat software that preserves the fidelity of all kinds of documents–including text and graphics–across a wide variety of computer platforms, printers, and electronic distribution methods. Adobe Acrobat is a family of universal electronic publishing software tools that allow users to create electronic documents that maintain the "look and feel" of the original–including all fonts and images–and can be distributed on electronic media including the World Wide Web, CD-ROM, and on-line services. The Free Acrobat Reader software lets users view, navigate, and print PDF files, and supports Windows 95, Widows 3.1, Windows NT, and Macintosh as well as DOS and workstation environments. Acrobat Reader software can be downloaded from Adobe's World Wide Web server at http://www.adobe.com/software.html and popular on-line services such as CompuServe and America Online. Adobe Exchange software is available for a wide variety of platforms for under $200 at popular computer retailers or mail order firms.

Pentium The fastest CPU chip being produced by Intel for IBM-compatible computers. Introduced in the fall of 1992, Pentium, originally named 586, is the successor to the 486 chip and uses a 64-bit internal bus, compared to 32-bits on the 486. The Pentium chip runs from half again to more than twice as fast as a 50MHz 486. Whether or not it is faster than the PowerPC chip remains the subject of much "my dog's better than yours" debate between aficionados of the Macintosh and IBM-based platforms.

peripheral Any external input or export device, such as a CD-ROM, removable media or tape drive, printer or scanner that is connected to a system. While *peripheral*, strictly speaking, refers to devices that are physically not part of the computer's housing, built-in CD-ROM drives have become so prevalent that such drives may be called a peripheral, even though it is part of the main computer box.

PET Personal Electronic Transaction. Introduced in 1977, the Pet computer was one of the first personal computers. It was a CP/M and floppy disk–based personal computer built by Commodore, who went on to create the innovative, but ill-fated, Amiga.

phosphor A rare earth material used as a coating inside the back of a **CRT**. When struck by an electron beam, a phosphor emits light for a few milliseconds. In color monitors, red, green, and blue phosphors are grouped into clusters called **triads**.

Photo CD A proprietary process of Eastman Kodak that places digitized files of photographs onto a **CD-ROM** disc. To get a Photo CD, all you have to do is take your exposed, unprocessed film to a photofinisher, who will turn your analog film images into digitized photographs. If you give them transparency film, you'll receive a box of slides along with a Photo CD disc containing all the images on the film. If you shoot negative film, you'll get a stack of prints along with the disc. Photo CD facilities can also digitize images from existing color slides and black-and-white or color negatives.

To produce a finished disc, a Photo CD Transfer Station converts your analog images to digital using a high-resolution film **scanner**, a computer, image processing software, a disc writer, and a color thermal printer. Each image is prescanned and displayed on the monitor. The operator checks the orientation (portrait or landscape) of the image, and begins a final, high-resolution scan. The digital image is adjusted for color and density.

Each 18MB photograph is then compressed to 4.5MB using Kodak's Photo **YCC** format image, and is then written to the CD. A thermal printer creates an index sheet showing the images transferred to disc and is inserted into the cover of the CD's jewel case.

Initially there were six different kinds of Photo CDs. Now a new, more flexible strategy has simplified the number of categories to two disc types: the Photo CD Master disc and the Photo CD Portfolio II disc.

The Photo CD Master Disc format is designed for 35 mm film. Each disc holds one hundred high-resolution images. The discwriter writes five different file sizes (and five different resolutions), which Kodak calls **Image Pac**, onto the CD. Resolution of the images is stated as the number of vertical by horizontal pixels a photograph contains. On a Photo CD Master Disc this is:

- Base/16 (128×192 pixels)
- Base/4 (256×348 pixels)
- Base (512×768 pixels)
- Base*4 ($1,024 \times 1,536$ pixels)
- Base*16 ($2,048 \times 3,072$ pixels)

The two smallest thumbnail sizes are used by digital image cataloging programs, and the base version is used for viewing on your monitor, television, or Photo CD and **CD-i** players. Base*4 is for high-definition TV, and the highest resolution is for photographic-quality digital printing. A subset of this disc type is the Pro Photo CD Master Disc, but anyone who shoots large-format whether they are an amateur or professional can use it. Besides 35 mm, Pro discs accept images from 120 and 70 mm rolls and from 4×5 sheet film. The Pro disc includes built-in copyright protection and offers a sixth, Base*64 resolution image that yields a size of $4,096 \times 6,144$ pixels. When an image is scanned, the processing lab enters the copyright information specified by the photographer and the text appears each time the image is accessed by a compatible software application. Copyright notification can't be removed even if the image is copied.

Until recently the only "gates"–that part of the Photo CD scanner that holds the film–available for Photo CD were 35 mm, 120, and 4×5 film formats, and these were the only formats Kodak's scanner would accommodate. Recently, Kodak introduced two new gates that make it possible to digitize more formats. The 645 gate allows 6×4.5 cm medium-format images to be digitized onto Photo CD, and the "Glass Gate" permits scanning of non-standard images such as panoramic 120, 6 x 12 cm, and some older film formats. At the 1995 Photo Marketing Trade show, Kodak announced a new scanner accessory for Photo CD work-stations that will allow photofinishers to scan **Advanced Photo System** film onto Photo CD discs.

Under a new licensing policy, any software or platform developer can obtain a royalty-free patent license for encoding and decoding images in Photo CD's Image Pac format. This policy will enable people to read and write Photo CD images as easily as other common graphic file formats, such as TIFF and JPEG, with the added benefit of cross-platform com-patibility. One of the first products that allows users to produce their own CD-ROM discs using Kodak's format is CD Creator 2.0 from Corel.

The second disc type is Photo CD Portfolio II disc, which replaces the former categories of Print, Catalog, and Portfolio discs. Portfolio II discs can contain Photo CD Image Pac files and any other digital content, providing a single disc type for customers in prepress, presentations, image archiving, and other applications served by the previous Photo CD disc formats. In conjunction with the new application strategy, Kodak introduced a software application that lets users write Photo CD Portfolio II discs using their desktop computers. Previously available only for UNIX, Kodak's Build-It Photo CD Portfolio disc production software will be available for the Macintosh and Windows NT.

Opinion: Kodak's Photo CD provides the lowest-cost, highest-quality scans you can find anywhere and is my first choice for scanning images because of:

- *Compatibility*: Photo CD may be the Rosetta stone of graphics files formats. The same disc containing your photographs can be accessed by any Macintosh or Windows graphics program that recognizes the format. With the recent unlocking of the format, that promises to be almost every graphics application.
- *Price*: It typically costs twenty-five dollars to digitize a 24-exposure roll of 35 mm film. If you have a large number of existing images to digitize, it's possible to cut a deal with your dealer for an even lower price per negative or slide. Whether you pay a buck an image or less, it's still much less expensive than purchasing a desktop scanner.
- *Flexibility*: Kodak's Image Pac format contains five levels of resolution. If you have images digitized using Kodak's Pro disc, you also have the option of adding a sixth file size with a resolution of

4,096 × 6,144 pixels. The Pro format even lets you mix and match Image Pac files, so you can choose to have some images digitized with the five basic resolutions and some with six. Having multiple resolutions on the same CD-ROM disc lets you work with a file size that fits the project and equipment you are working on, and allows you to jam as many images on the disc as you want. If only five resolutions are selected, a Master Photo CD disc holds one hundred images in any format. If you have all of your photographs created with the six resolution Image Pac, you can only store twenty-five images, regardless of film format.

- *Quality*: Kodak tells me that "the highest resolution level (4,096 × 6,144) Photo CD file captures all of the image data 35 mm film has to offer." Purists and pixel counters may dispute this but my experience has been that when using the highest resolution files on both the Master and Pro Master disks, I can produce magazine-quality images and negatives that can print large, exhibition-quality prints.
- *Space saving*: Each Photo CD disc can hold one hundred images. By comparison, if you have the same one hundred images scanned to the same resolution as Kodak's Image Pac format, it would require forty-one 44MB SyQuest cartridges or seven 270MB cartridges. Even if you used Iomega's new, inexpensive Zip disks, it would take eighteen of them to hold the same number of images found on one CD.

What's next? As part of Kodak's new digital direction, the company, along with IBM and Sprint, is working on improving the way computer users deal with images in computer networks. The traditional method of working with digital photos is based on sending a bitmapped image of a photograph. Kodak wants to change that by using three separate technologies, starting with the Photo CD format. Since an Image Pac formatted file stores photographs at multiple levels of resolution, network users will be able to work on-line with lower-resolution versions of an image, which transmit and display quickly, and can access the high-res version when it's required.

A second part of this is implementation of FITS (Functional Interpolating Transformation System). In January, 1995 Eastman Kodak Company and Live Picture, Inc. signed a technology and product development agreement covering a range of imaging applications. As part of the agreement, Kodak obtained a license to apply Live Picture's

Photo CD

Kodak's Photo CD system is a straightforward method for converting images from slide or negative film into a digital format that is readable on both Macintosh and PCs. Photo CD discs can also be viewed on a television set by using a Photo CD player, like the portable model shown.

resolution-independent image viewing and editing technology for future Kodak digital imaging products. FITS is a way of formatting and manipulating millions of pixels so that images are stored as a sequence of subimages (from full resolution to low resolution), which are organized into discrete "tiles" or segments, making it possible to quickly access only the information needed to fill the screen and rapidly manipulate the image. This unique algorithm treats changes to an image separately from the image file itself, allowing real-time image editing and faster transmission.

Lastly there's an Image Access System platform, which makes it easy for people to file and retrieve images from a central image server. Kodak is working to combine these elements into a single standard for sharing images across networks. This standard will extend the value of the current Photo CD Image Pac format by adding a script, based on the FITS algorithm, that allows edits to be transmitted independently of the image file.

Photo CD–Compatible A term applied to **CD-ROM** drives that tells potential buyers if that particular drive can read Photo CD discs. But what does that really mean? To use Photo CDs on your Macintosh or PC, your CD-ROM drive must be XA Mode 2-compatible. XA is short for Extended Architecture, which is an extension of the original CD-ROM standard and includes added capability for time-based data such as audio, video, and animations. Photo CD is based on Mode 2 technology of that standard. Since most CD-ROM drives these days are Photo CD-compatible only propeller-heads may be interested in these details.

If the box doesn't say "Photo CD-compatible" it probably isn't. PC owners will want a drive that is MPC2 (Multimedia Personal Computer, version 2) compliant. Besides being Photo CD-compatible, this means the drive is also double speed. A double-speed drive can transfer data from the disc to your computer at 300 kps (kilobytes per second,) double the original CD-ROM's speed of 150 kps. Mac owners will want a double-speed unit too, and triple-speed and quadruple versions are available from companies like NEC. In fact as I write this, quad-speed drives are rapidly becoming *de rigueur* for digital imaging computers. Lastly, the drive should be multisession capable. This is an ISO standard that allows information to be added to a CD-ROM disc that has already been written to. For example, when you take a roll of twenty-four exposures into your dealer and ask them to produce a Photo CD, you still have room for another seventy-six images. When you add images to that disc, it's called the second "session." Single session drives will only read the first session on the disc and ignore the rest.

Mac owners who can find certain non-compatible drives for a good price can make them Photo CD-compatible by installing FWB's CD-ROM Toolkit. This nifty product not only makes most non-compatible drives compatible, it speeds up the drive too. CD-ROM Toolkit won't make your single-session drive multisession compatible, but you can't have everything.

Photo CD software While almost all image enhancement and graphics software is compatible with Kodak's digital photo format, Kodak, itself, has produced a series of programs that make working with Photo CD images easy and fun. At base-level, you'll find Photo CD Access Plus for Windows and Macintosh computers. This package lets users open and display Photo CD images as well as crop, zoom, and rotate them. You can save photographs in other file formats so they can be used with image enhancement programs that may not currently support the Photo CD format. There's even a low cost version of Photo CD Access for DOS.

For more control over your Photo CD images, you'll want a copy of PhotoEdge. Available for both Macintosh and Windows, this $139 package lets you enhance your photographs by sharpening them or smoothing them for a softer look. PhotoEdge's brightness-and-contrast tool lets you control over- or underexposure, and there are tools that let you zoom, change perspective, rotate, mirror, or crop your images. PhotoEdge is a great program for computer users who don't need or want to do extensive manipulation, but would like to export photographs into desktop publishing programs.

If you have hundreds of images digitized, you're going to need some way to keep track of them. Kodak's Shoebox is one of the better image database programs available. This $345 Macintosh or Windows package helps automate the storage and retrieval of photographs by displaying thumbnails in a catalog that looks much like slides arranged on a lightbox. The program lets you assign caption and keyword data to each image so you can perform searches to find specific photographs or groups of photographs.

At the beginning of 1995, Shoebox was discontinued. Kodak immediately announced an upgrade path to Canto Software's Cumulus imagebase program. For $29.95, Macintosh Shoebox users can become Cumulus users. Since this is currently a Mac-only program, IBM-PC and compatible users have two choices: They can wait for the Windows version of Cumulus, which also costs $29.95 or for a limited time they can upgrade to Kodak's QuickSolve program for $99. Canto Software has promised a utility that will let Cumulus users convert their Shoebox catalogs into readable form.

Cumulus 2.5 includes many features that will benefit the new or experienced pixographer. The program includes a collection of image file filters permitting you to catalog the most commonly encountered image files and provides a filter generator allowing users to create generic filters that will support any document or file format. Loading images into a new or existing catalog file is a matter of using the Catalog command that quickly imports single images or multiple digital images stored in a folder or Photo CD. Cumulus also imports portrait Photo CD images in their proper orientation, something other imagebases don't always do. If you store some portrait images in landscape mode, the way that I do for photographs that will be printed on digital posters, Cumulus has a Rotate Thumbnail command to place the image properly in your catalog. Cumulus permits the use of tens of thousands of keywords to describe images stored in your database and an intuitive keyword screen allows you to create hierarchical keywords.

QuickSolve is an industrial-strength version of Shoebox originally designed for law enforcement and technical image management needs. It can open your Shoebox for Windows files directly, and when opened you will notice QuickSolve's toolbar provides access to frequently used imagebase commands. Using the program's TWAIN acquisition module, the program lets you import images from digital cameras or scanners. QuickSolve opens large Photo CD, including 80MB Pro format images, in seconds; and like any well-behaved imagebase program, QuickSolve accepts and organizes still video, audio, and even text and graphics files.

For multimedia fans, Kodak's Create-It lets even the most novice computer user produce presentations using simple, interactive menus and built-in templates. Arrange-It is an advanced program that creates complex presentations and can import files from applications like Adobe Photoshop and Persuasion, Lotus Freelance, and Microsoft PowerPoint. The major advantage Create-It or Arrange-It presentations have over other multimedia software is that finished programs can be stored on a Photo CD Portfolio II disc and don't require a computer in order to run. All you need is a Kodak Photo CD player (including their compact portable machine) and a monitor and you can view an interactive presentation complete with sound, graphics, and photos. Create-It is currently only for Macintosh computers for $245, while Arrange-It works with both Mac and Windows and costs $395.

One of the most exciting Photo CD software products is the Portfolio Disc Production Software which allows you to create your own Portfolio II discs using the Macintosh or Windows NT. Users will be able to create their own Portfolio II presentations right on their own desktop or use the software to store and distribute images in the Photo CD format. Adobe Photoshop users can, for example, import and edit Photo CD images and write them directly onto a Portfolio II disc along with their original images. Users can also choose the resolution of the images they distribute among the multiple choices offered by the Image Pac format. One of the software's coolest features is its ability to translate an image in any graphics format into the Image Pac format.

All this coolness comes at a price, however. The system requirements for the program are the most intense I've seen on any imaging product: 64MB RAM, a 2GB hard drive, SCSI acceleration card, and a double-speed CD writer to begin with. When all that's added to the $995 list price, it might be considered too expensive for some casual users.

photo-realistic Having a similar image quality to a conventional, silver-based photograph. Frequently used when describing the quality of **printer** output.

Photoshop (and Photoshop-compatible) While not the first, Adobe's software creation is certainly one of the–if not *the*–most popular image manipulation programs available. Originally created for the Macintosh, a Windows version followed the product's introduction, and it has become the image editing program of choice for many professional and amateur photographers. Part of the attraction is that while the program has very powerful capabilities, new users can use some of them without much training to create rudimentary correction in color, contrast and cropping. More experienced users will find that Adobe Photoshop has almost unlimited capabilities because of the **plug-in** architecture that Adobe designed into version 1.0.

Photoshop has become a de facto standard for all image-enhancement programs–Macintosh and Windows. It is rare to find any image manipulation program that does not support Adobe Photoshop-compatible plug-ins. Even desktop publishing programs such as Adobe (formerly Aldus) PageMaker and Deneba's Canvas 5.0 now support Adobe Photoshop-compatible plug-ins.

All of this power does not come without a price. Once you get beyond the basics, Adobe Photoshop quickly becomes complex. This has spawned a veritable cottage industry in Adobe Photoshop books and add-ons from many companies, including Adobe which publishes an excellent series of *Classroom in a Book* guides for Adobe Photoshop and some of their other graphics products. My advice to Adobe Photoshop wannabes is to remember that you didn't learn everything about photography (or graphics or design) overnight; it took time. You need to have the same expectations about using Adobe Photoshop. Practice and make mistakes.

Here's what service bureau Cies-Sexton's Kevin Elliott has to say on the subject: "You have to learn something new every day because if you don't learn something new on a regular basis, then you're going to stagnate, both creatively and technically. It's a constant learning process, and you must constantly update your skills and practice them to keep up to date; because once you're comfortable, you're behind."

PICT Another acronym without a strict definition, this time for a metafile file format. As a well-behaved metafile, PICT files contain both bitmapped or object-oriented information. Some people love PICT files because they are excellent for importing and printing black-and-white graphics, like logos. Others hate them because they don't always retain all of the information in the original image. I've had both experiences.

Picture Disk Kodak's new digital image on-a-floppy-disk service designed initially for use with the new **Advanced Photo System film**. The way is works for consumers is just like Photo CD: Users will simply request *Picture Disk* software when they take their Advanced Photo System film for processing by a Qualex authorized processing outlet. Qualex is a wholly owned subsidiary of Eastman Kodak and has thousands of retail outlets across the country, including some that may have names that do not specifically say "Qualex" or "Kodak."

The Picture Disk software and is available only for Windows, ending a long-standing practice at Kodak of developing for the Macintosh first. During the process, digitized images will be copied onto a $3\frac{1}{2}$-inch floppy disk which the user can then load onto their hard disk. Each disk will be able to store a maximum of twenty-eight digital images along with Picture Disk viewing software and a user's guide with detailed instructions. Unlike Photo CD, Picture Disk stores images at a single resolution—512×768 pixels—which should provide users with good onscreen quality and enough resolution for non-professional or FPO (For Position Only) graphics applications.

Picture Disk software allows users to perform basic image manipulation including viewing, cutting, pasting, deleting, rotating, cropping, resizing, and exporting. Other features include: slide show capability, the ability to create onscreen albums, and the ability to save files other file formats, including JPEG or Photo CD.

Pictures on Disk An alternative to Kodak's **Photo CD** process (and **Picture Disk** software, for that matter), created by **Seattle FilmWorks**, that places digital images onto a **floppy disk** instead of a **CD-ROM** disc. This process is the least expensive way to get reasonably high-quality scans of your new and existing images and is the one of the few systems (see **Picture Disk**) that delivers digital images on floppy disk. Since all PC owners already have a floppy disk drive, you don't need any new computer equipment.

Seattle FilmWorks processes all kinds of 35 mm film, including Kodak, Fuji, Agfa, and their own house brand of color negative film. If you're making photographs for exhibition or competition, you can use your new Nikon N90s, and if you're just shooting snapshots you can also create Pictures On Disk with any point-and-shoot or recyclable camera. After Seattle FilmWorks processes and prints your film, the images are scanned; each image file is approximately 900K in size. Before the file is saved onto a Pictures On Disk floppy, the photographs are compressed to 35K using a proprietary compression scheme developed by the Seattle FilmWorks. This .SFW format makes it possible to squeeze thirty-six exposures of image data onto a single 1.44MB 3½-inch floppy disk and allows for fast decompression of images.

It takes only three to five seconds to turn an .SFW file into a photograph on your 486-based PC's monitor. You can also order Pictures On Disk from existing images including 3½ × 5 or 4 × 6 prints, slides, or 35 mm color negatives. Similar types of images (negatives, slides, or prints) are digitized at the same time, so you can't combine prints, slides, or negatives on the same disk. You can even have Seattle FilmWorks crop an image from a print. If you do, be sure to include diagrams that show how you want each photograph cropped. Since there is more special handling with cropped Pictures On Disk, Seattle FilmWorks charges an additional five bucks per disk.

Because Seattle FilmWorks uses the .SFW format for delivering and storing images, you cannot read POD images without a copy of their PhotoWorks software. Fortunately, Seattle FilmWorks includes a two-disk set, containing both PhotoWorks for Windows and PhotoWorks for MS-DOS, at no additional charge with your first order of Pictures On Disk. PhotoWorks Plus, an enhanced version of the program, is available from retailers like Egghead Software for under $30. Along with the software, the package includes a single-use camera loaded with color negative film, a 24-exposure roll of Seattle FilmWorks private label film, and a prepaid film-developing certificate good for processing a roll of film, including prints, negatives, Pictures On Disk—and a free roll of film.

PhotoWorks Plus is an interesting image enhancement program that lets you create digital albums and screen savers, and will let you save your images in many common Windows and Macintosh graphics formats. As such, it's your "gateway" to other image enhancement programs. Photo-Works Plus lets you convert SFW files into the following graphics formats: CAL, CCITT, EPS, GEM, CompuServe GIF, JPEG, LEAD, MacPaint, Apple PICT, MS PAINT, OS/2 BMP, PCX, RAS (Sun Raster), TGA, TIFF and TIFF LZW (Compressed), BMP, WPG (WordPerfect), and WMP. You can perform basic image enhancements on your Pictures On Disk photographs and store the improved version on the same disk with the original image. At that time, you have the option of replacing the original image with the new one, or saving the enhanced version on the disk. In fact, if the disk isn't too crowded, you should be able to store both versions of some photographs on the disk. Because Photo CD is a Read-Only medium, it is impossible to save another version of an image onto a Photo CD disc but Pictures On Disk is an interactive process that lets you save, delete, and modify images the way you want.

piezoelectric The property of some crystals that oscillate when subjected to electrical voltage. A form of technology used by Epson in their Stylus Color **inkjet printers**. On the other hand, *piezo-electric* (with hyphen) technology generates electricity when mechanical stress is applied.

pixel Pixel is an acronym for *pic*ture *el*ement. A computer's screen is made up of thousands of these colored dots of light that, when combined, can produce a photographic image. A digital photograph's resolution, or visual quality, is measured by the width and height of the image measured in pixels. When a slide or negative is converted from silver grain into pixels, the resulting image can be produced at different resolutions.

All output devices, including monitors, are measured by resolution. The higher the resolution of an image—the more pixels it has—the better the visual quality. A Photo CD image with a resolution of $2,048 \times 3,072$ pixels has better resolution and more photographic quality than the same image digitized at 128×192 pixels. At lower resolutions, photographs have a coarse, grainy appearance that make it difficult to evaluate the image. A rule of thumb is that as the resolution of a device increases, so does its cost.

Pixels—the stuff digital photographs are made of—behave similarly to the silver grains that make up the negative or positive images in the film you use. Thinking of pixels as film grain will get you on the road to understanding how digital imaging works. If you look closely enough at any photograph, you will see silver grains. Isn't that what Antonioni's film *Blow-Up* is all about? When the hero enlarges the photo to mural-sized proportions, he is unable to tell if the object he is looking at is the murder weapon or several pieces of silver grain.

If you could look closely enough at a photograph on a computer screen, you would see the digital equivalent of grain—pixels. Pixels appear in clusters or **triads**. Each pixel is actually a combination of three colored dots placed close to one another. On the screen, combinations of these pixels produce the colors you see. A triad contains three dots, one each for red, blue, and green. In case you're wondering, that's why computer monitors are often prefixed with the letters RGB. In a typical RGB monitor three electronic "guns" fire three separate signals (one for each color) at the screen. If all three guns hit a single pixel's location, it will appear white on the screen. If none of the guns hit a target pixel, it will be black. The location and color of each pixel is also controlled by your computer. The number of bits of data associated with each pixel determines the visual quality of your photograph and is measured as **bit depth**.

pixel resolution Measures the number of pixels on a monitor.

pixographer A term coined by some would-be Lewis Carroll at a computer trade show to describe photographic artists who are taking George Lucas's quote to heart ("As digital imaging comes into wider usage, we are gradually moving this medium [motion pictures] away from a strict photographic interpretation of reality into one that is more painterly.") by creating images that extend Ansel Adams's concept of **previsualization** to digital imaging.

plug-in Plug-ins are little software applications that can be used to increase the functionality of and customize off-the-shelf graphics programs. You can think of plug-ins as additional blades or tools for your

Swiss Army knife, and selecting the right one can make a tough graphics job easier and a difficult job practical.

One of the main features of plug-ins is that they are easy to use and easy to install. All plug-ins are installed in the same way: They are simply copied into the "Plug-in" directory or folder of a program, and after that, they appear as menu items in that program. They are, in effect, "plugged in" to the software and after installation they become an integral part of it. The de facto plug-in standard was created by Adobe for their Photoshop image manipulation program, but Adobe Photoshop plug-ins can be used with many programs, including U-Lead Systems' PhotoImpact, Fractal Design Painter, Adobe Premiere, PixelPaint Professional 3.0, ColorStudio 1.5, and StataVision 3-D. *See* **filter**.

Plug-ins come in three basic types: Acquire, Functional, and Special Effects. Acquire plug-ins appear in a submenu of the Acquire item of your program's File menu. This submenu includes items that allow you to import or "acquire" an image that will be used by your graphics program. Since many Functional plug-ins relate to producing color separations, they usually appear in the graphics program's Export menu. Special Effects or image enhancement plug-ins appear in the program's Filters menu.

The popularity of Adobe Photoshop-compatible plug-ins is spreading to other programs. Adobe's latest version of PageMaker is now compatible with these plug-ins as is Deneba's Canvas 5.0 drawing program. Don't forget to cruise the graphic and photographic forums on CompuServe, America Online, and Prodigy, looking for plug-ins that can add functionality to your favorite program. For example, CompuServe has a great shareware plug-in that adds a large copyright symbol to your images.

If you already have Adobe Photoshop installed and decide to add a program like PixelPaint Pro, Fractal Design's Painter, or MicroFrontier's Color It!, here's a method to make those Adobe Photoshop-compatible filters and plug-ins do additional work. When installing Adobe Photoshop, you'll notice Adobe's Installer creates a number of additional folders (or directories) inside the Plug-ins folder (directory). They are called: Acquire/Export, Extensions, Filters, Displacement Maps, Parser, and File Formats folders. When installing third-party filters, it doesn't matter which subfolder (subdirectory) these filters are placed in as long as they are placed in the Plug-ins folder. I recommend you take all of your third-party filters and place them in a new folder inside the plug-ins folder and name it something personal, e.g., "Lauren's Folder." When using programs like

Painter, the installer asks you to specify where your plug-in folder is located. When it does, you can specify "Lauren's Folder," even though it's inside your Adobe Photoshop folder. Painter will then have access to these filters without having to install them on your hard disk a second time.

For PixelPaint Pro: Changes in versions 3.1 and later allow you to specify any folder as the official "Filters" folder, as you can do in Fractal Design's Painter. You can create an alias or simply refer back to a folder in Adobe Photoshop's plug-ins folder. For Color It!: Make an alias of your version of "Lauren's Folder," rename it as "Plug-ins," and place that alias inside the "Color It! Stuff" folder.

PMMU Paged Memory Management Unit. A chip for Macintosh computers that utilize the 68020 microprocessor, like the original Mac II or Macintosh LC. The PPM is built-in to the 68030 and later generation Macintosh **CPUs**. Macintoshes that have a PMMU can use the **virtual memory** feature of the System 7 (and later) operating systems.

PMT Photomultiplier Tubes are a type of sensing technology used in drum **scanners**.

PNP Plug-and-Play slots are similar to the ACCESS bus in their ability to communicate. This is the "next great standard" developed by Microsoft as part of the long-awaited Windows 95 operating system. Plug-and-Play slots allow the computer to recognize any card inserted into it through exchange of information. For the user this means lower setup costs, ease of use, and reduced need of technical support. Macintosh computers have always had plug-and-play capabilities, but Apple Computer never bothered to give a name to this feature.

port Some expansion cards have connectors that stick out the back of the computers. These connectors are called *ports*, and allow different external devices, like printers, to be connected to them. Sometimes these ports are built into the motherboard, which is almost always the case with ports on Macintosh and Power Macintosh computers. There are many kinds of ports and slots for both PCs and Macs. The size and number of slots determine the expandability of your computer.

portrait mode The orientation of a graphic or photographic image in which its shorter dimension is the horizontal side. The opposite is called **landscape** mode. Photographers would call this kind of photograph a *vertical* image.

PostScript A programming language created by Adobe Inc. that defines all shapes in a file as outlines and interprets these outlines by mathematical formulae called *Bezier* (Bez-e-ay) *curves*. Any PostScript-compatible output device, whether it's a film recorder or laser printer, uses these definitions to reproduce the image on your computer screen.

PowerPC A microprocessor that is the result of a joint IBM, Apple, and Motorola effort to make a **RISC**-based—and Intel competitive—computer system. It is a 32-bit multitasking microprocessor with an internal 64-bit data path similar to Intel's **Pentium**. PowerPC chips are the CPUs used inside Apple's Power Macintosh computers and certain IBM RS/6000 models.

power user Digital imagers, like skiers, can be classified into three groups—Beginner, Intermediate, and Advanced.

(The following definitions were inspired by definitions of different kinds of photographers found in Don Feltner's audio tape, *How to Make Money in Photography*, part of the Marketing, Advertising, and Promotions kit published by Studio Press. Contact Studio Press at 4330 Harlan Street, Wheat Ridge, CO 80033. Other sources of information and inspiration were a presentation given to the Macintech users group by Mike Phelps and Brad Tombaugh.)

A Beginner works alone in a small or home-based studio. Their software requirements include simple word processing, spreadsheet, and graphics apps. The Beginner usually spends two hours a day, or less, at their computer.

Intermediate users often work in groups, so networking solutions are important to them. Besides the above applications, these users are doing desktop publishing, working with shared scheduling programs, and using database managers. These people spend roughly four hours a day with their computers.

Advanced, sometimes called *Power Users*, spend more than four hours a day at their computer using profession-specific programs like Adobe Photoshop. These people need the fastest processors, the biggest hard drives, and make extensive use of peripherals like CD-ROMs, scanners, and modems. There are, of course, always exceptions to these classes, but most computer users/photographers fit comfortably into one or another of them.

PPA Professional Photographers of America. *Professional Photographer*, the official journal of the PPA, is the oldest exclusively photographic publication in the Western Hemisphere. It was founded in 1907 by Charles Abel. For information about the organization, contact them at 1600 The Healey Building, 57 Forsyth St. N.W., Atlanta, GA 30303. Phone 404/522-8600; fax 404/614-6405.

Benefits include: Networking–PPA connects you with a national network of unmatched industry. The Merit & Degree program provides continuing education for professional image makers through approved courses and competitions. PPA offers a number of insurance programs to its members, ranging from photography equipment insurance to major medical. Enrollment in PPA's valuable Indemnification Trust Program is automatic for photographers who join either the Portrait or Wedding Group. Members-only discounts on products and services from leading manufacturers and PPA '95 courses. Increase credibility to the general public through the PPA logo identity program. PPA is the leader in current information on copyright protection and related legislation. A copyright kit is available free to members upon request. The Certification Program for professional photographers, photographic specialists, and electronic imagers sets an industry standard. Marketing opportunities to increase your business potential are available through the Marketing Professional Photography and the "Once Upon a Lifetime" programs. All members receive a copy of the PPA membership directory, *Who's Who in Professional Imaging*. The directory is a valuable tool in helping contact other members for assistance, learning about other photography associations in your area, and finding vendors who offer supplies and services you might need for your business. Specific questions about any of these benefits and programs can be directed to the PPA Membership Department: 1-800-786-6277. (Benefit information courtesy PPA's forum on CompuServe.)

PPD file A PostScript Printer Description file is a file that contains information about a specific printer. PostScript *is* device-independent, but uses information in the PPD file to take advantage of features in the printer or imagesetter.

PRAM (Macintosh only.) Parameter Random Access Memory. This where the system defaults are stored along with any changes to system parameters. Since it is RAM and is volatile, PRAM is battery-powered to keep the information "hot." PRAM is similar to **CMOS** on the IBM-compatible computers.

TIP: If your Mac is acting strangely, one of the first things you can try to fix it is to "zap the PRAM." If the PRAM is corrupted by who-knows-what, zapping it—setting everything to zero—will usually solve your problems. If you are running System 7 or later, the way to zap the PRAM is to hold down the Command-Option-P-R keys as you start the system up.

precision transforms Also called PTs. These are device profiles defined as software and are used in color management systems.

PreP IBM's standard hardware configuration for computers using the PowerPC chip is called the PowerPC Reference Platform, or *PReP*. Apple Computer did not buy into PReP but has agreed to a later (and as yet unbuilt) specification called Common Hardware Platform or *CHRP*. Apple has promised that its next operating system, code named "Copland," will run on CHRP platforms regardless who builds them. In the meantime, a small Swiss company called Quix has been able to get Apple's System 7.5 running on a PReP specification computer. Yup. It's Macintosh software running on a real IBM computer. The only problem is that Apple has refused to license the Mac OS to Quix. Confused? Me too. Only time will tell when you will see Macintosh software running on an IBM-built computer. A year ago, I would have said "never"; today I would have to say "real soon now."

previsualization A photographic concept first outlined by Ansel Adams in the 1930s when he introduced a system of film development and printing that he called the Zone System. The heart of the Zone System is that photographers must plan both exposure and print processing when they make an image. The Zone System is based on how well the finished print matches the previsualized image the photographer had and *not* how well it matches what they originally saw when they captured the image.

This short definition is a gross oversimplification of, what can be, a complex process that for some photographers has achieved biblical status. There are many good books on the Zone System. My favorite is Fred Picker's *Zone VI Workshop*.

printer A peripheral device connected to a computer that produces paper-based (hard copy) output from data stored—and perhaps manipulated—by the computer user. Several kinds of photo-quality printers are available: **inkjet**, **laser**, and **dye-sublimation**. As is true in all aspects of digital imaging hardware, the higher the resolution of the device, the higher the cost. There are however two notable bargains: the Epson Stylus Color inkjet and Fargo FotoFun! dye-sublimation printers.

The Epson Stylus Color inkjet printer is an inkjet printer selling for less than $500 that claims to produce photo-realistic results. The Stylus Color's piezoelectric technology uses mechanical vibrations, instead of heat, to fire ink onto paper. Instead of the thermal approach favored by Canon, Apple, and HP, the Stylus Color places more uniform, consistent ink droplets and can deliver up to 720 dots per inch (dpi) resolution on specially coated Epson paper. It will also print text and color images at 360 dpi. Unlike some color inkjet printers, the Stylus Color uses two ink cartridges: one for black and one for cyan, magenta, and yellow. This means if you print a lot of text or black-and-white photographs, you only have to replace the black cartridge. Other inkjet printers mix all three colored inks and produce a muddy black. The Stylus Color is compatible with both Macintosh computers and PCs and has both serial and parallel ports built-in. For the PC, four scalable fonts and five bitmapped fonts are built-in.

It's a fact of life that while dye-sublimation printers provide the most photo-realistic output, they are also the most expensive. Fargo Electronics has managed to break the price barrier with it's new PhotoFUN! dye-sublimation printer which has an average street price of $399. The PhotoFUN! breaks the dye-sub price barrier by limiting the maximum print size to a snapshot-sized 4 × 6 inches. PhotoFun! is a compact printer that has a small footprint measuring approximately 7 × 9.5 inches.

PhotoFUN! has a three-color (CMY) ribbon with a fourth component that provides a clear UV coating to protect the prints from fingerprints and moisture. The printer comes packed with a 36-print ribbon and thirty-six sheets of paper. Installing the ribbon is no big deal, and there's a diagram inside the printer that shows you how. Wondering where you install the paper? Paper is fed in one sheet at a time and the driver tells you when to insert it.

The compact manual includes information for connecting the Photo-Fun! to either a Macintosh or PC. Connecting the printer is also simple: You plug in a printer cable into the serial port on the back of the computer and connect it to the printer. If you want to have more than one printer connected, you might consider an A-B box that will let you switch between the PhotoFUN! and your regular printer. The only false note in setup is the chunky external power supply that takes up a lot of space on your floor.

Prodigy An **on-line service** that is a joint venture of IBM and Sears and includes weather and stock market reports, airline scheduling, and at-home shopping. It's not currently as popular as CompuServe or America Online, but recently Prodigy has made major interface changes to make it one of the easiest services to from which access the **Internet** and **World Wide Web**.

program A series of instructions, written by programmers, used by computers to process data or images. Often called **software** or *software program*, although that latter term seems somehow redundant.

protocol The standards that apply to communications between computers and other devices on a network, or between computers and **on-line services** and **BBSs**.

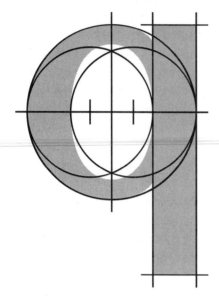

QIC Quarter-Inch Cassette. For some reason tape is more popular with Windows and DOS users than with Mac-heads but this is changing as multi-GB drives become less expensive and the thought of backing up these huge drives sinks in. The cartridges come in many different designations: there are QIC (Quarter-Inch Cassette), XL (long), and QW (wide-long) models, and variations on these names that sound more like the latest model BMW. The variety of tape formats may hinder acceptance, but the kicker is that the data is stored on the tape in serial form instead of the random method used by all other forms of removable media. When coupled with the inherently slower access time, magnetic tape has never gotten the respect it deserves.

Tape has one major feature that will endear it to thrifty computer users—it is cheap and provides the lowest cost per MB storage of any removable media. This makes tape the ideal medium for people who use their removable media drives for back-up or archival purposes.

There are many different tape drives available, here are a few of the more interesting ones: For removable storage and back-up of my PC, I installed an internal Jumbo 350MB Colorado Memory Systems QIC-80 tape drive. It's an inexpensive way to do backups and save image data for transportation to service bureaus. The internally mounted Colorado Memory Systems Jumbo 350MB tape drive has a street price of $140, and an external unit, called the Trakker 350, is also available. At $15 a cartridge, this medium is currently the least expensive way to back up your hard disk. Colorado Memory Systems is a division of Hewlett-Packard.

Iomega created the Ditto family of drives providing internal and external models in 250, 420, 850, and 1700MB capacities. All the drives carry a five-year warranty and use direct drive, so there's no belt to stretch or break. Iomega's Ditto 250 and 420 have street prices of $99 and $149.

Quadra Apple's brand name for Macintosh computers that use Motorola's 68040 microprocessor chip. With the introduction of the Power Macintosh series of RISC-based computers, the Quadras have disappeared from the product lineup, although they were—for their time—a capable and competent computer for digital imaging.

queue This is not a line that Britishers stand in to catch the bus or Captain Picard's nemesis—it is just a temporary holding place for data in your computer. A queue can also be a stream of tasks waiting to be executed; for example, documents waiting to be printed are said to be queued.

QuickTime Apple's multimedia **extension** that adds sound and digital video capabilities to apps that have been designed to take advantage of it. A QuickTime file can contain up to thirty-two tracks of audio, video, or **MIDI** information, and some image-enhancement programs require the extension's built-in **compression** capabilities. Many database and **imagebase** programs also support QuickTime. Apple has also designed a version for Microsoft Windows.

QWERTY A standard typewriter keyboard is called QWERTY because the top row of letter keys on the left side spell the "word." Computer keyboards typically have twenty to thirty more keys more than standard typewriter keyboards, and many of these additional keys are called *function* keys, e.g., Control, Escape, and Apple's Command key.

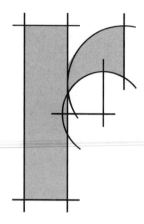

RAID No, this isn't an aerosol spray can that's used to get bugs out of your computer. It's really a Redundant Array of Inexpensive Disks. This is a type of disk drive that is actually *two or more drives* working together to provide increased performance and improved levels of error recovery. Once expensive, these RAID units costs have plummeted along with all **mass storage** devices.

RAM Random Access Memory. RAM is that part of your computer that temporarily stores all data while you are working on it. Unlike a floppy disk or hard drive, this data is volatile–if you lose power or turn off your computer, the information disappears.

Most contemporary computer motherboards feature several raised metal and plastic slots that hold RAM in the form of **SIMMs** (Single In-line Memory Modules). Although the more RAM you have the better, there are economic considerations too. Having more memory slots means having the ability to use more of the less-expensive SIMMs, instead of fewer, more costly ones.

The software that runs the computer and enables you to do digital imaging requires a minimum amount of RAM. If you don't have enough, the computer displays an error message that says, in effect, "TILT." One rule of thumb in figuring out how much RAM you need is to get as much as you can afford and twice as much as you think you need. If you want more concrete numbers than that, make a list of the programs you plan on using. Then, go to your favorite software store and check out at the minimum memory requirements (listed on the boxes) for the programs that you want to use. Since both Macintosh's Finder and Windows allow you to have more than one program open simultaneously, think about what combinations you might be working with at the same time. Add up those numbers and throw in a couple of megabytes for elbow room, and that's what your memory requirements should be. If you're serious about digital imaging, having less than 16MB on either a PC or Mac will create bottlenecks when working on digital photographs. An important rule of thumb when working with digital images, is that you can never have too much memory. The Power Macintosh 8100 computer I'm writing this on has 24MB installed, and I don't seem to run out of memory anymore.

raster (1) A pattern of horizontal lines on a TV screen illuminated by a beam of the CRT when data is input. The illuminated dots (pixels) produce visible images.

(2) Raster graphics: A technique for representing an image as a series of dots or pixels. Unlike television, which uses a single raster standard, there are many graphics standards for both Macintosh and PCs and image enhancement programs. *See* **Bitmap**.

rasterize The act of converting **vector graphics** images into **bitmaps** so that they can be displayed on a monitor or printed. With the exception of plotters, which use vector images directly, all non-bitmapped images must be rasterized for **output**.

read-only memory This that part of your computer's memory that cannot be changed by a user. The contents of a **ROM** chip (or chips) on a motherboard are permanent and contain information entered by the manufacturer that software accesses to accomplish operations in a standard and consistent way.

read/write head A device, part of *all* disk drives—either floppy, hard, or removable—that reads and writes data onto a disk or tape.

red book *See* CD-ROM.

refresh rate Often called *vertical scanning frequency*, this measures the amount of flicker you see on your monitor. A computer screen, like a TV set, is constantly reenergizing its phosphors. To display at resolutions higher than 640×480, the monitor must have a horizontal scan rate of at least 35 kilohertz, or kHz. (Hertz is a measure of electrical vibrations. One hertz equals one cycle per second.) The standard refresh rate is 60 Hz, and at this speed your screen is redrawn sixty times per second. Higher frequencies mean the image has more stability and better display quality. If the refresh rate is too slow, you get flicker. Sixty Hz is standard but flicker may be apparent in some larger, brighter screens. That's why many monitors have now standardized on 70Hz, and some go as high 87Hz. New and more expensive graphics cards support higher vertical scanning frequencies, like the 72Hz European standard. Make sure your graphics card supports the refresh rate of your monitor.

removable media Removable media drives are computer peripherals that use data-holding cartridges that can be easily removed from the drive and have many advantages for computer users, especially digital photographers. Sometimes called *removable hard drives*, they are more correctly called removable media, since the media being removed might be optical as well as magnetic. People use them for many different things: They can make backups of the data on your **hard disks** and, next to a **modem**, they're the cheapest way of transporting data from point A to point B. Without removable media, digital photographers wouldn't have a way to take large image files back and forth to their **service bureaus**. Placing financial data on removable media and locking it in a safe-deposit box provides a level of security even the most ardent hackers can't breach.

The performance of fixed or removable drives is measured by **seek time** or **access time**. Seek time is the amount of time required for the arm of a direct access storage device to be positioned over the appropriate track.

Access time is the interval between a call for data and the completion of data delivery. Some pundits are convinced that the only relevant measurement is *sustained transfer rate*, which measures the average number of bytes per unit of time passing between disk storage and processor storage. The truth is that a fast drive is usually just as fast no matter how you measure performance.

Up until recently, the most popular magnetic cartridge drives are from SyQuest Corporation, which has corralled over 90 percent of the removable magnetic media market. SyQuest drives and cartridges use off-the-shelf hard disk components housed in a proprietary plastic shell. This technology, often called "**Winchester**" after IBM's original hard disk with two 30MB disks, was adopted by SyQuest in 1982. SyQuest and similar magnetic media-based drives are almost as fast as the fastest hard drives, and are less expensive than an equivalently sized optical drive.

One of the most interesting removable magnetic drives is the Bernoulli box. Unlike a traditional hard disk in which read/write heads float over a rigid disk, the Bernoulli disk is flexible (it's made of similar material to floppy disks), and at high speeds bends to be close enough for the head to read it. During a power failure, a hard disk must retract its head to prevent a crash, whereas the Bernoulli floppy naturally bends away. Another new removable magnetic drive is called Jaz. Unlike Bernoulli, Jaz devices use fixed instead of flexible disks, and have been designed to hold 1GB of data. Both Bernoulli and Jaz drives are made by Iomega Corporation.

Optical removable media drives are more properly called *magneto-optical*, and a laser is used to heat the disc and thus change its reflectivity to produce media that can be erased and reused. One of the negatives of optical drives is that writing data to optical media requires three spins. The first erases existing data, the second writes new data, and the third verifies the data is there. When compared to magnetic drives, all this spinning tends to reduce performance.

render To draw a real-world object as it actually appears. Here's how it works in practice: Programs, like MetaTools Bryce, create graphics in the form of **wireframes**. Wireframes are a method of representing three-dimensional shapes and objects as if they were constructed out bits of wire or pipe cleaners. In order to see your landscape as a completed image, it must be *rendered*. Rendering is when color, shading, and shadows are applied to the wireframe in order to produce a realistic appearance. How quickly this happens will depend on the size and complexity of the image and the power of your computer.

resolution A digital photograph's resolution, or image quality, is defined as an image's width and height as measured in **pixels**. When a slide or negative is converted from silver grain into pixels, the resulting digital image can be made at different resolutions. The higher the resolution of an image—the more pixels it has—the better the visual quality. An image with a resolution of $2,048 \times 3,072$ pixels has better resolution and more photographic quality than the same image digitized at 128×192 pixels. At lower resolutions, digital photographs often have a coarse, grainy appearance that makes it difficult to evaluate an image when looking at it onscreen. Unfortunately, a rule of thumb is that as the resolution of a device increases, so does its cost.

RGB Red, Green, Blue. Color monitors use red, blue, and green signals to produce all of the colors that you see on the screen. If you've ever made Type R prints from slides in your own darkroom, you're already familiar with working with the additive color filters of red, blue, and green used by computers. If so, the RGB setup used by computer monitors should make perfect sense to you. If not, the concept is built around how different colors of light blend together.

RIFF Resource Interchange File Format. A multimedia file format introduced by IBM and Microsoft that allows audio, image, animation, and other elements to be stored in a single file.

RIP While I am writing this definition on Halloween, it does not mean Rest In Peace, but rather Raster Image Processor. RIP is a process that prepares image data for the screen or printer. Before dye-sublimation printers print images, they first save a temporary RIP file to disk, which is then used to print the final output. RIP files rasterize specific types of data, such as PostScript or vector graphics images, as well as different kinds of bitmapped data.

RISC Reduced Instruction Set Computing. RISC chips, like the PowerPC, are programmed with fewer, simpler instructions. Since they break each operation down into small, simpler steps, the computer can perform these operations faster. The Power Macintosh models use a RISC microprocessor chip from Motorola instead of the 68000-based Complex Instruction Set Computing (**CISC**) chip used in most Quadra and Performa models. RISC chips are faster than CISC and can be designed and built more economically.

ROM Read-Only Memory.

RSC The device-independent reference color space used by color management systems to establish the characteristics of a particular color device.

RS-232 A standard 25-pin connector used to connect a computer to a modem or other **peripheral** devices. For IBM AT-style expansion boards, a 9-pin connector is used.

RTF Rich Text Format. A file format, originally developed by Microsoft, for encoding text and graphics. It was adapted from IBM's DCA file format and supports **ANSI**, **IBM** PC, and Macintosh character sets.

saturation Saturation, often referred to as *chroma* by show-offs, is a measurement of the amount of gray present in a color. *See* **HSB**.

save To retain the data contained in any kind of file by copying it to a floppy or hard disk or any kind of removable media. Since RAM is volatile, an unsaved file will disappear when the computer's power is turned off.

scan (1) To convert an image from hard copy form into a **bitmapped** digital form, or to convert characters into **ASCII** text.

(2) In a monitor, to refresh a **CRT** display. *See* **refresh rate**.

scanner We're not talking about David Cronenberg's cult horror film masterpiece, but those useful hardware peripherals that convert original text, artwork, or film into digital form. Scanners accomplish this by passing a light-emitting element across your original and transforming the analog image into a group of pixels that is ultimately stored in a digital file. There was a time when scanners were so expensive only large advertising agencies and service bureaus could afford them. Now, scanners have a wide range of prices to fit everyone from the casual snapshooter to the independent designer to people interested in electronic document management. As prices have dropped, scanners have become an indispensable peripheral.

Scanners come in three basic types: Hand-held scanners let you do all the work by rolling the scanning element across the face of your original. They have the advantage of being inexpensive but the disadvantage of being limited by the scanner's head width. Some hand-scanners include software that allows you to "stitch" separate scans together. How well this process works depends on the steadiness of your scan and the software itself. Hand scanners are great for the occasional scanner, but if you want better results you'll need to get a desktop scanner.

Sometimes called *flatbed* scanners, they look like small copy machines, and there are similarities in how they work. Depending on design, they automatically make one or three passes across an original lying flat on a piece of glass.

A new class of scanners has appeared whose only purpose is the processing of paper for OCR purposes or grayscale photographs for digital imaging use. There are not many of them, but if you're looking for a low-cost scanner for photographic purposes, this may be just the product you need. One of the most popular is Visioneer's PaperPort for Mac and PC. This hybrid scanner features an ease-of-use that makes it almost as easy to use as a hand scanner but it's no-nonsense design and capabilities place it closer to a flatbed. There's no off-on switch; it turns itself on when you insert a print, and turns off when a scan is completed. A scan takes about six seconds. It can read documents as small as a business card or as large as 8.5 × 30 inches. Both versions use a serial connection, and the drag and drop scanning software offers three modes: normal text, fine print, and photo.

Traditionally, scanners use a **CCD** (Charge Couple Device) array consisting of several thousand elements arranged in a row on a single chip. Three-pass scanners use a single linear array and rotate a color wheel in front of the lens before each of the three passes are made. A single-pass scanner uses three linear arrays, which filter red, blue, and green light.

The same image data is focused onto each array simultaneously. When scanning an original photograph or artwork, a single pass scan is all most people require, but when scanning secondary, printed, or copied material, a three-pass scan will usually remove the inevitable moiré or dot pattern. Flatbed scanners come in different resolutions and the one that's right for you will be the one the matches the resolution and quality of your final output. For most users, a flatbed scanner is the answer, but film scanners allow you to scan negatives and transparencies in much the same way as flatbed scanners. They are more compact and their cost and design is based on the different film formats they scan. Pick the one that fits the maximum film size you use but be aware that one key feature you will be looking for in a slide scanner is *dynamic range*.

A scanner's dynamic range depends on the maximum optical density that can be achieved and the number of bits captured. In simple terms, the greater the density range (4.0 is ideal) the better the scanner. Until recently, only expensive slide scanners offered a density range over 2.5. Now more affordable scanners can perform at 3.0 or higher. By comparison, a Photo CD scan has a dynamic range of 2.8. Scanners are measured by their *optical* as well and *interpolated* resolution. Optical resolution refers is the raw resolution produced by the scanner's hardware, while interpolated resolution uses software to add pixels to simulate a higher resolution. Digital purists scoff at the concept of interpolated resolution as a marketing gimmick and insist that optical resolution is the only meaningful representation of a scanner's real capabilities. As in any photographic equipment purchase, you need to analyze your needs and budget vis-a-vis the hardware specifications before making a final decision. And as always, do a test, if you can, before plunking down your hard-earned cash.

I think that scanner software is often more important than the hardware. One of the most important developments is the **TWAIN** standard that allows compliant software to scan text or images directly into an application. Unless the scanner is easy to use, regardless of how high its resolution may be, you will not be able to get usable results. This is especially important if you plan on using your scanner for *optical character recognition* (OCR) of text. When shopping for scanners, my recommendation is that you base 60 percent of you decision on software and the rest on hardware specifications.

Scrapbook (Macintosh only.) A permanent system file that can holds frequently used text and graphics, as compared to the Clipboard (which Microsoft Windows also has, but not a Scrapbook), which contains similar graphics or text data as long as the computer is powered up.

screen saver A software program that, after a user-specified amount of time, launches and displays some kind of dynamic graphic on your screen to temporarily replace the spreadsheet, database, or image enhancement program you were working on, but stopped. There was a time when your computer really needed a screen saver. If anything stayed on your monitor too long, it would "burn" into the screen's phosphors, leaving a "ghost" image. Screen saver software prevented this from happening with ever-changing onscreen images that prevented the phosphors being incinerated. Today's use of resilient phosphors make screen burn-in highly unlikely, and we probably don't need screen savers at all. But that doesn't mean we don't want them.

Screen savers have become a fashion statement. The kind of screen saver you use says a lot about the kind of person you are. They proclaim your college alma mater, vocation, musical taste, or attitude. Screen savers quickly passed from Johnny-One-Notes and nowadays include many different modules in the same package. This is why most packages are called *collections*. The screen saver's engine lets you run your favorite module or several selected modules using a random setting after a user-specified amount of inactivity. Since contemporary screen savers are multimedia extravaganzas, full of sound and animation, the potential exists for system conflicts. Most of the popular packages should give you no problems, but other users may have the opposite experience. More often, the problem may be one of hard disk space. Sound and animation files, gobble it up and programs like Delrina's *Opus 'n Bill on the Road Again* screensaver packages takes 7MB out of your hard disk. Since hard disk prices are at all-time lows, this may not be an issue with most users.

SCSI It means Small Computer System Interface but is pronounced "scuzzy." SCSI is an 8-bit computer interface that allows for the connection of up to seven **peripheral** devices to a single SCSI port. SCSI has been a standard connection port on all Macintosh computers since the introduction of the MacPlus in 1986 but not on the IBM-PC platform.

PC owners must install a SCSI expansion board, or SCSI controller in order to attach a SCSI device to their computers.

SCSI-2 This is a 16-bit implementation of the SCSI bus. This standard provides maintains compatibility with the older SCSI standard while providing the ability to transfer data at rates up to 10MB per second—twice as fast as the older SCSI specification.

Seattle FilmWorks Since 1976, Seattle FilmWorks has been providing 35 mm photofinishing services and related products on a direct-to-consumer basis. In 1994, they produced the first affordable and convenient service for digitizing photographs onto floppy disk instead of CD-ROM disks. Called **Pictures On Disk**, this service is a spin-off of the lab's work in digital imaging.

Seattle FilmWorks is a mail-order photo lab that has developed a method for digitizing a roll of 35 mm negatives and placing them on a floppy disk—instead of a CD-ROM. With a customer's first order, the lab includes a copy of PhotoWorks Plus, a Windows-based image enhancement program. As I was completing this book, the company introduced a Macintosh "Lite" version that gives Mac users access to the images on the floppy disks. *(Photo by Joe Farace)*

seek time The performance of fixed or removable drives is measured by **seek time**, or the amount of time required for the arm of a direct access storage device to be positioned over the appropriate track.

selection tool One of the most important tools found in an image enhancement program are selection tools. These allow you to highlight or select portions of an image that will have an effect applied to them. Most programs offer three types of selection tools: Marquée, Lasso, and Magic Wand. The Marquée is used when you want to make regularly shaped selections. Double-clicking the Marquée tool opens its control palette and lets you choose either a rectangular or elliptical selection shape. The Lasso is a freehand selection tool you can use to outline irregularly shaped objects. You can also use it to create Polygons by pressing and holding the Option key (PC users should use ALT) and clicking on various points around a subject. For more information on the Magic Wand, see **Magic Wand**.

To assist with the selection process, Adobe Photoshop's Select menu offers additional commands that increase the efficiency of whatever tool you may be using. The Grow command, for example, temporarily doubles the Tolerance range for the Magic Wand. Another way to increase the selection being made is to use the Similar command. When you do, the program can select all other colors that fit within the specified Tolerance.

serial port An outlet on the back of a computer used to connect peripheral devices such as modems and printers. The serial port sends and receives data one bit at a time.

service bureau This is a term left over from the bad old days of computing when only the high priests and their acolytes had access to computers and few "real" people could afford to own one. Instead, they had to take their data—in punched-card form—to companies who did own computers and who, for a fee, would process their data for them. Today's service bureau can digitize your analog photographs using scanners or Kodak's **Photo CD** process or turn digital images into analog form, including prints, slides, or negatives.

A service bureau can take many forms. It can be a small specialized facility that only provides Kodak Photo CD service, or a large commercial lab that offers a wide range of digital input and output services. Some service bureaus cater to the prepress market and can provide four-color separations directly from your Adobe Photoshop or PageMaker digital files. The key to using any service bureau is not too different from finding the right professional color lab–

Compare: Talk to your photographer friends and find a service bureau that can provide the services you need at a price you can afford. While price alone is not a major consideration, it *can* be used to compare facilities that offer a real standard product or service. In my area, I can pay $3.00 or 70¢ each for a Photo CD scan. Photo CD Pro scans range from $4.00 to $18.00. In each case, my experience with the lowest cost Photo CD provider has been as good as the highest price.

Test: When a photographer gets a new piece of equipment, the first thing he or she does is shoot a test roll of film. That's also a good idea when dealing with service bureaus. Take a representative group of images and divide it into two groups. Send one to one service bureau and one to the other. Many companies like Adobe and Kodak offer coupons for a small number of free Photo CD scans. Use these coupons for a risk-free test of a service bureau.

Evaluate results: When the images or scans come back, evaluate the entire experience, not just the quality of the service bureau's output. Were the scans/files delivered when they told you they would be? Is the price the same that was quoted? After that look at the results.

Decide: Once you've made a decision, stick with that service bureau through thick and thin. People who change labs frequently are never satisfied with the results. All labs–and all a service bureau is really nothing but a digital photo lab–make mistakes. What differentiates a good one from a bad one is not just the quality of their product, but how they treat you when they make a mistake. What you need to know is how quickly they correct their mistakes and how they treat you during the process.

shadow mask A thin screen that is attached to the back of a color monitor screen. The mask has small holes through which an electron beam is aimed onto the **phosphor** dots that form on-screen images.

shareware Shareware is a creative way of distributing software that lets you try a program for up to thirty days before you're expected to pay for it. The registration fees for shareware are usually quite modest, ranging from five bucks to one hundred dollars. (Some authors just ask for a postcard, or "beer and pizza money," or donations to a specified charity.) As a thank-you for your payment, authors often will send you a printed manual, an enhanced version of the program, or a free upgrade–or, at no charge, additional products they've developed. **Freeware** is a form of shareware that is just what it sounds like–it's free.

SIGGraph Special Interest Group for Graphics. A non-profit organization devoted to computer graphics and sponsor of a large trade show focusing on graphics hardware and software products.

SIMM Single In-line Memory Module. A SIMM is a group of memory chips mounted on a small plastic card, and its capacity is measured in bytes, such as 1MB, 4MB, 8MB, 16MB, and 32MB. SIMM slots vary in number and depend on the size of the case and motherboard. Some Macintosh models have only one SIMM slot, while other Macs and PCs will have as many as eight. These little "sticks of chips" vary in price depending on demand, world market conditions, phase of the moon, etc.

slot Often called Bus Slots. They accept printed circuit cards that allow accessories or devices to be attached to the **motherboard**. These cards are the equivalent of interchangeable lenses for your computer, and depending on what type of card is inserted in the slot, allow the computer to accomplish different tasks. As with interchangeable lenses in photography, there are many kinds of cards manufactured by many different companies. Selecting the card to do the job you want is comparable to deciding which manufacturer's 35–70 mm lens you should add to your camera system. To find the right lens, you read product reviews in magazines and talk to your friends about their experience with theirs. Do the same thing with cards.

In order for input and output devices to function, they must be physically attached (by cables) to a card inserted into a slot. In the PC world, you will find 8-bit, 16-bit, and 32-bit slots, and, depending on the motherboard design, you will find one or two of each slot type installed. One way to identify the different kind of slots is that as they go from 8 to 16 to 32 bits, the slot gets longer. Inside a Macintosh you will find NuBus, PDS (Processor Direct Slot), and, in the latest models, PCI slots. A NuBus card automatically tells the CPU what its function is, but a PDS slot is passive and is used for specific functions, like the board that allows the Macintosh to emulate the PC environment.

SMPTE Society for Motion Picture and TV Engineers. SMPTE is a professional society that prepares standards for film and television production. For synchronization purposes, SMPTE developed a standard time code that is used to record hours, minutes, seconds, and frames on motion picture film or audio or videotape.

software The instructions that a computer needs in order to operate. Like many contemporary cameras, there are two main functional ingredients in a computer system: **hardware** and software. One is useless without the other. Software is the list of instructions that enable hardware to function as it was designed. On a modern camera, for example, the LCD display panel on top that shows aperture and shutter speed is part of the camera's hardware, but it's the camera's software that tells that display what f-stop the lens is set on and what shutter speed has been selected.

SoftWindows Insignia Solutions offers a software-only solution to *emulating* the Windows environment on a Power Macintosh. Since SoftWindows is software, it doesn't tie up a **PDS** or **NuBus** slot, and is less expensive. SoftWindows emulates an Intel 486 chip and performance is scaleable, e.g., the faster your Power Mac is, the faster SoftWindows will run. In general, the current version of the program will produce performance similar to a 25MHz 486SX IBM-compatible computer. The latest SoftWindows requires a 16MB Power Macintosh computer but all the Mac's RAM is available when the emulation isn't running, and you can use Apple's Virtual Memory or Connectix's RAM Doubler without problems. SoftWindows supports all Apple monitors and third-party monitors, like my NEC XE15, that work with the Mac and PCs. Soft-Windows also provides full Windows sound support, but not **Sound Blaster** compatibility. Depending on your application, that may or may not be a problem. If networking is a consideration, SoftWindows is fully network aware when using Ethernet, Token Ring, and AppleTalk.

SoftWindows is the ideal solution for the Power Mac owner who needs to run one or a few PC-only products. Software emulation is inherently slower, albeit cheaper, than hardware emulation, but I've found Soft-Windows is great for running a program like PhotoWorks Plus from **Seattle FilmWorks**. This program runs slower on my Power Mac than on my 486 machine, but I am able to use the program with other Macintosh graphics programs and swap images between the two environments by copying images onto the Mac's clipboard and pasting into a Mac application. The same would be true for other Windows-only apps like CorelDRAW!, Lotus Notes, and Novell's PerfectOffice. Insignia Solutions will be offering its own upgrade to Windows 95.

Sound Blaster A family of sound cards from Creative Labs, Inc. The Sound Blaster standard is so popular that it has become the de facto audio standard for PCs.

sound card A personal computer **expansion board** that can record and play back sound, as well as provide output jacks for the connection of an external amplifier or multimedia speakers. Some sound cards also include **MIDI** capability. The three major standards for the PC world—sound has been built into the Macintosh since it was introduced in 1985—are **Sound Blaster**, Ad Lib, and Windows. Some cards support all three, but Windows emulation software, like SoftWindows, only supports Windows sound standards.

Not so long ago, the only computer users with external speakers were those people with Sound Source's audio utility, which made their computers sound like *2001*'s HAL. All that's changed. Macintosh and IBM-compatible machines now bundle CD player software that also lets you listen to musical CDs. As I write this, I'm listening to the music of Beethoven from the soundtrack of the film *Immortal Beloved*. It sure beats radio—and there are no commercials. CD player software exploits your CD-ROM drive's ability to play music CDs, but external speakers make multimedia presentations and games more interesting and fun too.

Shopping for speakers may seem a daunting task. Where once there were only a few, inexpensive speakers, there are now products that span the spectrum from cheapie to audiophile. To help you make a decision, here's a checklist of the major features your multimedia speaker should have:

- *Magnetic shielding*: Without shielding, speaker magnets can cause interference when placed next to your monitor. Shielded speakers can also prevent damage to data on your hard disk or removable storage media.
- *Amplification*: Get amplified speakers. Unamplified speakers cost less but there is a vast different in performance. Microsoft Windows 95 has improved the audio output from some sound boards, like my 16-bit Sound Blaster, but powered speakers make games and

multimedia sound better, with less distortion. Many speakers are battery-powered but my experience is that batteries don't last long and an inexpensive power supply quickly pays for itself. Please note that many speaker systems, although powered, do not include an AC adapter. Expect to pay $8–10 for an adapter–especially for lower priced speakers.

- *More Power!*: The "more power" axiom doesn't apply to computers as it does to home audio. Powered speakers' output varies from one watt per channel to twenty watts and since the average user sits close to their computer, three to five watts per channel is more than enough power. On the other hand, if you plan on using your speakers for presentations to audiences of fifteen or more people, make sure that you have at least ten watts per channel.
- *Frequency response*: Just as in home audio, the frequency response of your PC's speakers is important. An ideal response is 40Hz to 20KHz, and mid- to high-end speakers usually fall into the 70Hz to 20KHz range. If you anticipate working in the MIDI environment, consider speakers with greater dynamic range that have separate woofers or subwoofers to handle the music's bass or low-end frequencies. These kinds of speaker systems are more expensive, but the sound quality is impressive.
- *Check the controls:* A good speaker system will have a master volume control and adjustable tone controls to let you tweak the bass (low) and treble (high) frequencies to match the acoustics of the room you keep your computer in.

When shopping, look for all these features and make sure you listen to the speakers before taking them home. Most computer showrooms have less than optimum acoustics, so bring your own music CD and listen to several systems before picking the one that sounds best to you.

SPA The Software Publishers Association is an industry-sponsored organization that offers a variety of educational materials about the do's and don'ts of copying software. Copying software that doesn't belong to you is illegal and immoral. The SPA calls this practice "piracy," but you and I know it by another word–*theft*–and the SPA actively prosecutes violators of piracy laws. The basic rule of software ownership is that you should own one copy of a program for each machine it runs on. If you use Adobe Photoshop, you must own one copy of that program for each computer it is installed on. For more information, contact SPA at: 1730 M Street, NW, Suite 700, Washington, DC 20036, or call 202/452-1600.

spreadsheet A program that simulates a paper worksheet in which columns of numbers are summed. A spreadsheet appears on screen as a matrix of rows and columns, and data is entered in boxes (formed by these intersections) called cells. The most popular spreadsheet for both Macintosh and Windows is Microsoft Excel.

stylus (1) A pen-shaped tool that—when used with a graphics tablet—can draw images as well serve being able to use as a mouse substitute.

(2) A **photo-realistic** color **inkjet** printer made by Epson USA. *See* **Printer**.

SYLK Symbolic Link file. A spreadsheet file format that Microsoft developed for its pre-Windows spreadsheet program Multiplan, still is widely used by a number of other spreadsheet programs.

SyQuest Some of the most popular magnetic removable drives are from SyQuest Corporation, which has corralled over 90 percent of the removable magnetic market. SyQuest drives and cartridges use off-the-shelf hard disk components housed in a proprietary plastic shell. This technology, often called "**Winchester**" after IBM's original hard disk with two 30MB disks, was adopted by SyQuest in 1982. SyQuest drives are almost as fast as the fastest hard drives, and are less expensive than an equivalently sized optical drive. The cartridges, on the other hand, are more expensive than the optical equivalent. The other disadvantage, which SyQuest shares with all removable drives, is that because the cartridges are removable, they are more difficult to seal against dust and environmental hazards like cigarette smoke. For that reason, SyQuest recommends the use of a removable dust shield on the front of their drives.

SyQuest offers a five-inch, 200MB drive that can also read and write 44MB and 88MB cartridges and a three-inch 270MB drive compatible with their now discontinued 105MB cartridges. The older-design 200MB drive has a seek time of 18ms, access time of 27ms, and average write transfer rate of 1.8MB per second. The same statistics for the newer, faster 270MB drive are: 13.5ms, 22ms, and 2.1MB per second. SyQuest introduced a low-priced 135MB removable drive called EZ135 and has announced a 1.3GB SyJet drive that should be widely available by the time you read this. The greater penetration of SyQuest products in the graphics industry means that both products should get wide acceptance.

SYSOP A SYSOP is the System Operator of a BBS or forum on an on-line service. On a large forum, there may be several Sysops, each with expertise in different areas. You can send messages to the Sysop through **e-mail** or through the forum's message section.

system disk A hard or floppy disk that contains part or all of the computer's operating system. In the PC environment, the MS-DOS system disks have two hidden files and the COMMAND.COM file. In the Macintosh environment, a system disk contains the System Folder.

system folder (Macintosh only.) This folder contains the System and the Finder along with printer drivers, fonts, system **extensions,** and **control panels**.

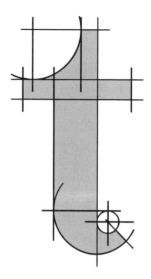

tape A form of removable media that moves magnetic tape past a read/write head, much like an audio cassette deck does with audio tapes. Unfortunately, magnetic tape is truly the Rodney Dangerfield of removable media. The reasons magnetic tape drives "don't get no respect" are varied. The variety of tape formats may hinder acceptance, but the real problem is that the data is stored on the tape in serial form instead of the random method used by all other forms of removable media. When coupled with the inherently slower access time, magnetic tape has never gotten the respect it deserves.

Tape is distinguished by the fact that it's cheap. It provides the lowest cost per MB storage of any removable media. This makes tape the ideal medium for people who use their removable media drives for backup or archival purposes.

TARGA Not Porsche's topless model, but TrueVision Advanced Raster Graphics Adapter, a **raster** graphics file format developed by TrueVision, Inc. for its line of (originally) PC-based video graphics boards used for high-resolution digital imaging. Targa files are identified by a .TGA file **extension** and handles 16-, 24-, and 32-bit color information.

terabyte One trillion (or ten to the twelfth power) **bytes**. While once the stuff of science fiction, terabyte-sized hard disks are on their way now in the form of hard disks for desktop computers.

thermal dye-transfer Often called **dye-sublimation**. A printer type utilizing a printing head that heats a dye ribbon to create a gas that hardens into a deposit on the special paper used by the printer. Like most printers, it prints in the form of "dots" of colors, but because these dye spots are soft-edged (as opposed to the hard edges created by laser and inkjet printers) the result is smooth continuous tones.

throughput A way to measure a computer system's productivity that is based on specific performance over a fixed amount of time. For example, a printer's throughput is typically measured in pages per minute.

thumbnail This is an old design-industry term for "small sketch." In the world of digital photography, thumbnails are small, low-resolution versions of your original image. Since they are low resolution, they produce extremely small files.

TIF, TIFF Tagged Image File Format is a bitmapped file format developed by Microsoft and Aldus. A TIFF file (.TIF is the extension is used in Windows) can be any resolution from black and white up to 24-bit color. TIFFs are supposed to be platform-independent files, so files created on your Macintosh can (almost) always be read by a Windows graphics program.

TIGA Texas Instruments Graphics Architecture. A graphics standard developed by Texas Instruments that provides a resolution-independent interface between a program and the graphics **coprocessor**.

tint *See* **hue** and **HSB** for details.

toggle To alternate back and forth between two situations inside a given software program. A program may allow you to *toggle* back and forth between an image in color or black and white. This switching can be done with keyboard commands or mouse clicks.

tool palette A collection of on-screen functions (such as Crop, Magic Wand, Paint Bucket) that are grouped together into a single, unified menu structure to allow users easy access to the controls. Most image enhancement and graphics programs sport tool palettes. One that makes the most extensive use of tool palettes is Fractal Design's Painter.

As soon as you launch Painter, you know you're not in Kansas anymore. This program's interface is dramatically different from most manipulation and enhancement programs and its seven palettes are collapsible—so you can keep those that you often use scattered around the screen. Serious Painter users may wish to consider adding another monitor to display tools and palettes, or to get a larger monitor. Here are a look at a few of the available palettes:

- *Brushes*: Contains icons for five different tools from a pencil to charcoal and sports a "pushbar" that when clicked expands the palette to offer variants of that tool. Fractal Design calls this the "secondary" palette and they can be "torn off" (and placed anywhere on the screen) if you have more than one secondary palette available at a time. A pop-up menu also provides six to ten variations on the brush used. If you can't find it here, it doesn't exist.
- *Tools*: This palette contains the kind of basic tools you'd expect to find in any image enhancement program and includes Brush, Paint Bucket, Magnifier, and an assortment of selection tools.
- *Control*: This is a companion palette to Tools. When you select a new tool from the Tool palette, the Control palette changes to present the specific options for that tool.

toolbar Some image enhancement programs, like Seattle FilmWorks, eschew tool palettes in favor of a row or column of buttons that can activate the application's various functions. Sometimes the toolbar is movable so it can be placed close to the image being manipulated and users can move quickly between different options. Some toolbars, especially in Microsoft applications, can often be customized allowing buttons to be added and deleted.

trackball A pointing device—a mouse alternative, if you will—that contains a movable ball rotated with the fingers or palm. Unlike a mouse, a trackball is a stationary unit; you just move the ball and click mouse-like buttons adjacent to it. Apple Computer introduced a built-in trackball in its PowerBook line of laptop computers and almost overnight it became the de facto pointing device to be included in a portable computer.

transfer rate The performance of fixed or removable drives is measured by **seek time** or **access time**. Some computer users are convinced the only relevant measurement is *sustained transfer rate*, which measures the average number of bytes per unit of time passing between disk storage and processor storage. The truth is that a fast drive is usually just as fast no matter how you measure performance.

triad A computer screen is made up of many thousands of pixels and pixels appear in clusters called *triads*. Each pixel is actually a combination of three colored dots placed close to one another, one each for red, blue, and green. On the screen, combinations of these pixels produce the colors you see.

true color The ability to generate photo-realistic 24-bit color images that include up to 16,777,216 colors.

TrueType TrueType is a successful attempt by Apple and Microsoft to introduce scalable **font** technology into the Macintosh and Windows environments. TrueType fonts look good both on screen and when output from either a **PostScript** or non-PostScript printer. Unlike PostScript fonts, TrueType fonts have only one component and have a slightly different icon so you won't get them confused with bitmapped fonts. It's generally acknowledged that TrueType was developed to wrest the chokehold Adobe had on the font market. It must have worked, because after the introduction of TrueType, fonts started to get cheaper. For more details on TrueType, see the **fonts** section.

TWAIN TWAIN is a hardware/software standard that allows users to access scanners from inside Windows applications. In addition to scanning, typical TWAIN software allows users to adjust brightness and contrast.

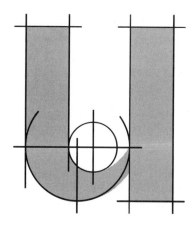

UMA (PC only.) Refers to RAM in the part of the first megabyte called the Upper Memory Area in that part of the computer's memory between 640K and 1MB

unbundle To sell components in a hardware or software package individually. If a system includes a monitor and the buyer wants to substitute another (especially more expensive) monitor, the dealer will *unbundle* the monitor that was originally included as part of a package.

Undo One of the most useful tools, commands, and/ or features an image enhancement program can have; it lets you go back to the way the image was *before* you made the last change. Unlike working in a wet darkroom, the undo command makes it possible to try new techniques without permanently changing an image and thereby encourages exploration and experimentation. Some programs include Undo as a menu item or keyboard command—most often Command-Z (on the Macintosh) or CTRL-Z (in Windows). Some programs, like **Seattle FilmWorks Photo-Works Plus**, have an Undo button on its **toolbar**. This tool looks like a left-hand U-turn arrow.

Some image editing programs have many (up to twenty-eight is not uncommon) levels of Undo that essentially allow the user to reconstruct the original image from all of the operations performed since opening the file.

UNIX A multi-user, multi-tasking (doing more than one thing at the same time), multi-platform operating system originally developed by Bell Labs for mainframe and mini-computers back in the bad old days of computing. Like the Internet, UNIX is constantly being overhyped as "the next big thing." Its main popularity now seems to be in universities and some large businesses, and while there are many implementations of UNIX for PCs and the Mac, none have caught on. The main reason is that the operating system requires large amounts of memory and **hard disk** space.

unsharp mask A technique provided with some image enhancement programs to—get this—*sharpen* a photograph. This oddly named function is a digital implementation of a traditional darkroom and prepress technique in which a blurred film negative is combined with the original to highlight the photograph's edges. In digital form, it's a more controllable method for sharpening an image. Here's how it works:

The first thing I recommend you do with any Photo CD image is sharpen it. While Adobe Photoshop provides a Sharpen menu and Sharpen command, I suggest you use Unsharp Mask because the dialog box includes a preview window that allows you to see the sharpness of the finished image before it's sharpened. Unsharp Mask gives you a movable "hand" you can use to choose the portion of the image that will allow you to easily see the effect of your sharpening. Further preview controls include Plus and Minus sliders underneath the preview window. Clicking on the Plus box zooms into the image, and clicking on the Minus box zooms the preview window out. To control the amount of sharpness, the dialog box provides three sliders that let you control sharpness and unsharpness. Sliding the Amount slider displays the actual percentage of sharpening that will be applied to your photograph, and don't be afraid to apply more than 100 percent to the highest-resolution Photo CD image. The preview window continuously updates the effect of sharpening on the image, so keep moving the slider until the preview looks as sharp as you want.

upgrade (1) HARDWARE: to improve some aspect of your computer system, e.g., swapping a 100MB **hard disk** for one that has a capacity of one **GB** *upgrades* the system.

(2) SOFTWARE: When Adobe announced that Adobe Photoshop 3.0 was replacing the previous version (2.5.1), registered owners were able to upgrade to the new version for a cost less than purchasing a new copy of version 3.0. Adobe Photoshop users were then able to upgrade the software to the latest version of the program.

UPS No, this isn't United Parcel Service, but instead is Uninterruptable Power Source (or Supply). This is a battery-operated power supply that you plug your monitor, computer, and peripherals into. It automatically switches on when your office or studio power goes off–or drops to an unsustainable voltage level. Most photographers would never go on-location without a backup camera body, but what about their computers? Purchasing a UPS may not be as much fun as getting new software or a faster processor, but like a backup body, it could save you a lot of time and money.

uptime The time in which your computer system is working properly–as compared to downtime, when the system isn't working at all.

URL Universal Resource Locator. The technical term for the location of a **home page** on the World Wide Web. For example, the URL for *Photo> Electronic Imaging* magazine's home page is: http//www.peimag.com.

UseNet User Network is a public access area on the **Internet** that provides news and e-mail.

utility This is not your local power company but a small, useful program (often **shareware** or **freeware**) that provides enhancement–if only cosmetic–to your system software or image enhancement program. One of the most popular utilities for the Macintosh is Now Utilities 5.0, a collection of utilities that enhance finding files and managing folders and extensions. A popular package for both Macintosh and PC users is Norton's Utilities, which provides the ability to resurrect files that have been deleted as well as managing the health and well being of your hard disk. The utilities that you have installed on your system help customize it to exactly how you want your system to look and function; you can't live without a great collection of utilities.

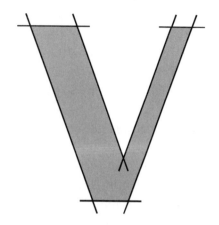

Variations A command found in Adobe Photoshop that gives you control over the hue and color intensity of an image. Similar features are found in other graphics programs, such as DeltaPoint's Graphics Tools, under "Test Strip" and similar names. Experienced darkroom and color lab workers will recognize it as the digital equivalent of the "ringaround" methods for producing test prints and test strips. Here's how it works in Adobe Photoshop:

When working on a photographic image for the first time, one of the most important steps is making sure the image's color and saturation are what you want it to be. The easiest and fastest way to accomplish this is by using the Variations command in Adobe Photoshop's Image menu.

When Variations is selected, you will see a large dialog box displaying "before and after" preview windows in the upper left-hand corner along with ten more previews. The first seven windows display the original image in the center, while the surrounding pictures show what the image will look like when more red, blue, green, yellow, cyan, and magenta are added. The intensity of the color corrections is controlled by a slider allowing you to go from Fine to Gross. All you need to do is look at the image you like best and click on it. Instantly, the original image in the center will be updated, and the before and after images in the left-hand corner are updated to reflect any changes. There are also three vertical preview windows that allow you to lighten or darken the image. More fine tuning is available through radio buttons above the Fine/Gross Slider. These buttons give you control over an image's Shadows, Midtones, Highlights, and Saturation. Again, it's just a matter of looking at the previews and selecting the one that looks best to you. Experienced darkroom technicians will recognize this process as a "ringaround" in which different densities and filter packs are applied to a test print to find the one that works best. Unlike a ringaround, Adobe Photoshop's Variations is instantaneous and if you don't like the effect after you've clicked OK, you can always use the program's Undo command to start all over again.

vector Images saved in this format are stored as points, lines, and mathematical formulae which describe the shapes that make up that image. When vector files are viewed on your computer screen or printed, the formulae are converted into a dot or pixel pattern. Since these pixels are not specified as part of the file itself, the image can be resized without losing any quality. Photographs are not typically saved in this format.

Some computer users, especially Mac users, call vector-format files *object-oriented* and you will often see that term used on graphic drawing programs. Vector files use the same technology that Adobe uses with its PostScript fonts and has the same advantages—you can make any image as big as you want, and it will retain its quality. Vector graphics are displayed as a **bitmapped** graphics on your monitor.

VESA The Video Electronics Standard Association set standards for high-resolution video devices such as monitors and video circuits. VESA also developed a standard for IBM-compatible machines called VL-Bus (VESA Local) for video boards and slots that can be plugged into the motherboard.

VGA The Video Graphics Adapter (or Array) is the minimum video display standard for Windows computers. A standard VGA system displays 640×480 pixels to display 16 colors at one time. At 320×200 pixels, the monitor can show up to 256 colors. Third-party manufacturers later increased resolution and numbers of colors to Super VGA, which provides a resolution of 1280×1024 with sixteen million colors.

IBM introduced this standard in 1987 when it launched the PS/2 system. Unlike previous video standards, VGA had the potential to display millions of colors. Not all VGA systems display this number, however. How many colors they can display is dictated by a particular adapter's design. A standard VGA system displays 16 or 256 colors at a resolution of 640×480 pixels. This resolution is the same as a typical consumer television set and often a good TV, like a Sony XBR, looks better than your computer because it has better **bit depth**.

Because monitors look like television sets, many computer users get confused when shopping for a monitor. For instance, when you trade-in your 19-inch for a 30-inch Sony, you expect to see the same image you saw on your old TV, except bigger. This doesn't happen with monitors. With a larger screen, greater resolution is possible. This enables you to see *more* of the same image. A 15-inch monitor can display a 800×600 pixel image, while a 19-inch model lets you see $1,280 \times 1,024$ pixels. Like televisions, monitor manufactures overstate the screen size somewhat. NEC is honest enough to admit that their XE15 15-inch monitor has a 13.8-inch viewable area.

Other than screen size and resolution, the next most important factors in evaluating your choice of monitors is **dot-pitch**, **refresh rate**, and whether the monitor is **multiscan** or **interlaced**.

video capture One of the least popular methods of image acquisition is using hardware and software that can "capture" an on-screen image from videotape into a graphics file format that can be handled by an image enhancement program. Video capture boards and software are often called "frame-grabbers" because they grab a frame of videotape and store it on your hard disk. This method is not as popular as other forms of image acquisition because the average frame-grabber product produces an image that is typically lower in resolution than could be produced by a scanner or digital camera—but, and it's a big but, video capture techniques are the only way to take an image from videotape and create a digital image from it. A video capture board also provides a quick and easy way to capture low- to medium-resolution images from a video camera or camcorder.

Here are a few examples of frame-grabbers: Play Inc. offers its new Snappy video capture module that looks like the easiest-to-install desktop video product available for Windows computers. All you have to do is plug the compact module into the parallel port of your PC, connect a camcorder or VCR to it, and when you see what you want on your computer's screen, simply click "Snap" and the software freezes the video. The bundled software includes a mixer that can enhance the images after you've captured them.

Another interesting PC-based video capture product is Media Cybernetics MRT VideoPort Imaging Systems. The resolution of the digitized image can be adjusted up to 768 × 768 pixels, the maximum resolution of a standard **PAL** video signal. What's unusual is that the board is available as a **PCMCIA** card that can be installed in any laptop or notebook computer. Also bundled with the board is Imager software that can enhance captured video images as well as scanned or Photo CD photographs.

video driver A small software program that enables your computer and video card to communicate with the monitor.

virtual memory This is a means of using **hard disk** space as if it were RAM. If you're working with a digital imaging program that require more RAM than you have installed, Windows will go to your hard disk and grab the amount of space you need—as if it were RAM—and use it to temporarily store data.

You may have heard that image manipulation programs are memory hogs and in order to work with photographs or graphics files you need to have a large hard disk and lots of RAM. That's partially true but it's also where virtual memory can come to your rescue. Image enhancement programs like Adobe Photoshop require memory that is three to five times the size of the image in order to work on a file. This means you need between 54 and 90MB of RAM to handle a 18MB file.

Adobe Photoshop has a built-in virtual memory scheme called "scratch disk" that reduces RAM requirements by treating your unused hard disk space as additional RAM. In order to use the program's scratch disk feature there should be enough room on your hard disk space for your other software and for Adobe Photoshop's virtual memory. The program's

Preferences menu lets you specify where the program should go to get this hard disk space, and you can designate primary and secondary disks to use as scratch disks.

If you don't have enough memory or scratch disk space, Adobe Photoshop will give you a "Not Enough Memory to Complete that Operation" error message, and this often occurs after the program has been working for a while. Fortunately, there's an easy enough way to keep tabs on memory while you're working on a graphic image. In the lower left-hand corner of any picture's window, Adobe Photoshop displays information showing how much memory that particular image takes. By clicking on these numbers, you have the option of displaying File Sizes or Scratch Sizes. While the File Size information is interesting, I recommend you keep the window set to show Scratch Sizes. That's because the number on the left side will tell you how much memory all open windows are using and the number on the right tells you the amount of RAM available. If the first number is larger than the second, the difference is the amount of Scratch Disk space required.

virtual reality Computer software and hardware that places users into an artificial three-dimensional environment produced by a computer. It requires the use of a unique kind of gloves, headphones, and stereo scopic glasses (or a helmet) that lets you see and manipulate this artificial space and its objects as if you were really there. Current virtual reality simulations are crude but keep getting better and better. We are still miles and years away from the level of realism found on the *Enterprise's* holodeck.

virus Viruses are small, invasive programs written by malicious misfits (usually referred to as **hackers**) that are designed to create havoc within your computer systems. You can get computer viruses in the same way that you get the human variety; through contact with another, contaminated computer. It's possible that such contamination can be introduced into the manufacturing process, but although I have heard of a few cases, it is quite rare.

There is software to protect your computer from viruses. If you plan to swap disks with other photographers or members of a user's group, the first software program you should install should be virus protection program. One of the most popular Macintosh virus remedies is a freeware program called Disinfectant, which is available through BBSs and most online services.

VL VESA Local Bus. *See* **VL bus**.

VL bus Stands for VESA Local Bus. VESA means Video Electronics Standard Association. This is a group of industry manufacturers who set standards for high-resolution, high-performance video devices. VL bus cards will not work in an ISA slot.

VLF Very Low Frequency radiation produced by computer monitors. *See* **EMF** for details.

VRAM Video Random Access Memory. In all Macintosh systems and in some PC systems, the video card function is built into the motherboard, but space is provided for Video Random Access Memory **SIMM**s. There is a separate set of memory chips in some computers that affects pixel resolution and the number of colors displayed. In PCs this memory is contained on a separate video board. You must have enough video memory to address all the pixels on the monitor multiplied by the number of bits of color resolution per pixel. For example, an 8-bit video system displaying 256 colors requires twice as much memory as a 4-bit per pixel system displaying sixteen colors at a time. Some computers allow you to expand display capability by installing additional VRAM to increase color depth. Like standard memory, the more VRAM you have, the merrier. Additional VRAM provides greater bit depth and is usually so inexpensive, I recommend that you spend the few dollars it takes to have the maximum amount installed when you purchase the computer.

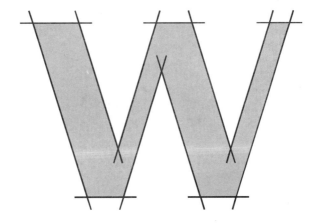

Wallpaper A pattern or picture used to represent screen background in a graphical user interface such as Microsoft Windows or the Macintosh. Mac users call this feature Desktop Patterns. Most system software includes several wallpaper patterns, and many third parties offer packages that include screen savers and wallpaper.

web site An Internet location (with an often-cryptic URL address) on the **World Wide Web** that will contain a home page for a company, organization, and with increasing frequency, an individual. Consider it a combination meeting place and electronic storefront. It's a place where people and organizations leave information about themselves and visitors can ask questions—and get answers to them.

wide bandwidth A communication channel that can transmit data—including images, sounds, and video—

at high speeds. The opposite is **narrow bandwidth** channels that can only transmit at slow speeds.

Winchester This original **hard disk** technology is often called "Winchester" after IBM's original hard disk design that employed two 30MB platters.

window An on-screen, rectangular, scrollable viewing area that is part of a graphical user interface, such as Microsoft **Windows** or the Apple Macintosh operating system.

Windows More properly called Microsoft Windows, this was an attempt to make the DOS command-line interface more user-friendly by providing a graphical user interface. Unlike the Macintosh GUI, Windows is more accurately an operating *environment* instead of an operating system, since it still required that users have Microsoft's DOS installed. This requirement vanished with the introduction of Windows 95, which no longer requires DOS (after installation), but does provide access to a DOS-like environment for use of older non-Windows apps.

The original Windows was introduced in 1985, but it took until the creation of Windows 3.0 in 1990 for this operating environment to really become the de facto standard for IBM-compatible computers. When Windows 3.1 was introduced, the die was cast.

wireframes A way of representing three-dimensional shapes in which all surfaces of the object are depicted in lines, including internal components normally hidden from view. When viewed on screen, wireframe objects appear as if they were constructed out of bits wire or pipe cleaners. This allows graphics programs to manipulate the object faster and more easily than if the image was fully rendered.

WMF Windows Metafile Format. A vector graphics format designed to be portable from one PC-based program to another.

World Wide Web One of the most popular aspects of the Internet, the World Wide Web has a set of defined conventions for publishing and accessing the information using **HyperText** and multimedia. Seemingly, the WWW contains everything you ever wanted to know about anything.

While there are interest groups for everything from mountain climbing to Porsche sports cars, there is plenty of marginal information on the Web too. It was bad enough to see CyberSex and hate groups railing against Barney the dinosaur, but now Coors Brewing has opened a **home page** on the WWW for Zima drinkers. Here's just the place where legions of Generation X fans of this soda pop–like alcoholic brew can chill out, join "Club Zima," and ask questions about how this pseudo-beer is made.

WORM   (1) Write Once Read Many times. A type of optical disk or CD-ROM that can be recorded only once. The CD-ROM version is often called CD-R (Compact Disc-Recordable).

   (2) A form of computer virus that continually duplicates itself on your hard disk, gradually using all of your computer's resources before ultimately shutting it down. Fortunately, worms are not as popular as they used to be—possibly because they are complex to create—but unfortunately, viruses are still with us. Just yesterday, my wife reported that her office computer—a DOS-based PC—had become infected.

WYSIWYG   Pronounced wissy-wig. As Flip Wilson's Geraldine used to say—and it had nothing to do with computers—"What You See Is What You Get." This term refers to the ability to view text and graphics on screen the same as they will appear when printed. While most test and image-processing programs have WYSIWYG capabilities, not all do. Read the fine print when you think about purchasing any program. A GUI is useless unless the apps that run under it are fully WYSIWYG.

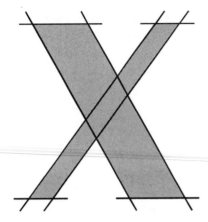

Xaos Tools (Pronounced "chaos.") A software company that offers several packages of Adobe Photoshop-compatible **plug-ins** that can produce striking images. Paint Alchemy is a Macintosh-only product that lets you use many different built-in effects or you can create your own. There are 101 preset brushing styles that can apply special effects such as Pastel, Ripple, Vortex, Threads, Smoke, and Bubbles. Their latest version of the package, which is accelerated (**native mode**) for the Power Macintosh, features a new interface with easy access to all settings for brush stroke coverage, color, size, angle, and opacity. You can even animate the effects and export them as QuickTime video clips using Adobe Premiere or Equilibrium's DeBabelizer. One of my favorite effects, Bubbles, might take twenty minutes to accomplish using Adobe Photoshop's standard controls, but Paint Alchemy achieves the same effect within a few minutes.

XGA A type of video adapter developed by IBM for the PS/2 computers. It puts out a resolution of 1,024 x 768 pixels (more than two and one-half times what's possible with VGA) with 16-bit colors allowing it to display 65,000 colors.

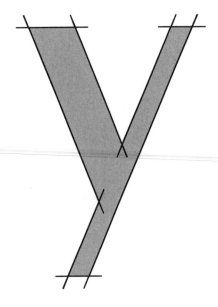

YCC The color model used by Kodak in its **Photo CD** process. This involves the translation of data that was originally in RGB form into one part of what scientists call "luminance" but the rest of us call *brightness*–this is the Y component–and two parts, the CC, of *chrominance* or color and hue. This system keeps file size under control while maintaining Photo CD's "photographic" look. Sony uses a similar system in its professional Betacam video system.

yellow book *See* CD-ROM.

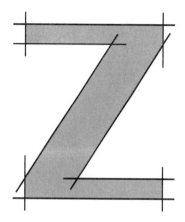

ZFP Zero Foot Print. This term is used to describe peripherals that take little or no additional desk space when installed. Often this means they are designed to sit under an existing peripheral or the computer itself.

Zip Iomega's Zip removable media drive has a street price under $200, and uses a propriety combination of Winchester read/write heads and **Bernoulli box**-like flexible disks to produce an average seek time of 29 ms. Pocketable, preformatted Zip cartridges, scarcely larger than a floppy disk, are less expensive than SyQuest. Bundled software for Mac and Windows computers includes backup, file cataloging, disk duplication, and management utilities that feature read/write disk locking, formatting, diagnostics, and hard drive emulation. Iomega also includes Guest software, which permits temporary use of a Zip drive on other computers.

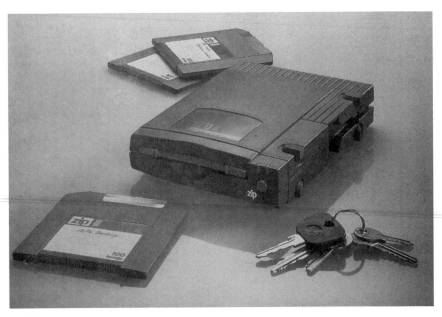

Iomega's Zip drive combines the compact size and functionality of a floppy disk with the capacity of a removable media drive and is available for both Macintosh and IBM-compatible computers. Zip also combines hard disk features with Iomega's Bernoulli box to provide an inexpensive storage media for digital images. You might consider it digital film.

zoom (1) A tool found in most image enhancement programs—most often by an icon in the shape of a magnifying glass. Zoom is depicted by this icon so often that this tool is often called "magnifying glass." This tool lets you zoom into a photograph by clicking your mouse's button. On the IBM-compatible versions—which often use a two- or even three-button mouse—you zoom in (make a section of the image *larger*) by clicking the left-hand button, or out (make a section of the image *smaller*) by clicking the right-hand button. This is especially useful when viewing a portrait photo in landscape mode. It's usually a good idea to zoom in before rotating it to its proper orientation.

(2) A company that makes inexpensive yet powerful modems. My Power Macintosh is connected to a 9600 bps external Zoom modem, while my Prime-built PC has a 14,400 internal Zoom modem.

appendix A

Which computer is right for you?

The first step in purchasing your first computer or upgrading the one you already own is establishing the *configuration* your computer will have, regardless of which platform (Mac or PC) it will be. The size and type of components used in a system define a computer's configuration. If you need additional equipment, what kind should it be? To help make your decision, I've prepared a checklist that will guide you toward making an intelligent purchase. If you don't understand the jargon or buzzwords used, please refer to the rest of the book.

How much memory do you need?

One rule of thumb in determining how much RAM you initially need: Get as much as you can afford and twice as much as you think you need. Another way to figure out memory requirements is to make a list of the type of programs you plan to use. Generally, business-oriented programs, like spreadsheets and word processing programs, take less RAM than photographic imaging apps. Go to your favorite software store and look at the minimum memory requirements of the programs you think you need. Since both the Macintosh's Finder and Windows 95 allow you to have more than one program open simultaneously, think about what combinations you might be working with at the same time. Also keep in mind that the system software, the program that lets you interface with your computer, occupies RAM too. Microsoft recommends a minimum of 4MB for Windows 95, and a color Macintosh system requires at least the same amount of space. Add those numbers and throw in a couple of megabytes for elbow room—that's what your memory requirements should be. Under no circumstances should you buy any computer with less than 8MB of RAM, and in a short time you'll probably need more.

How big a hard disk do you need?

To determine your hard disk requirements you can use a similar procedure. Check the hard disk space requirements for all the programs that you would like to have. Unlike memory, where you may only have one or two programs active at one time, apps sit on your hard disk, just waiting to be called up. The corollary to my RAM rule of thumb is that you never have enough hard disk space to add the program you just bought. And that's becoming a big problem. In recent years, software has exploded in size, and even a word processing program like WordPerfect 6.0 for Windows grabs 18MB of disk space.

I expect the trend toward "fatware" won't abate in the near future, so add up the hard disk requirements of the programs you would like to have, add 25 percent for turnaround space on the disk and see what the result is. And don't forget the system software. On my Power Macintosh, my System Folder takes 60MB of space and even my PowerBook laptop takes 18MB. Just like RAM, buy as large a hard disk as you can afford, but if you plan to work with digital images, never get one smaller than 500MB. Most likely a gigabyte or multi-gigabyte drive is what you need. The good news is that unlike RAM prices, drive prices have steadily declined as hard disks grow bigger and faster.

What about floppy disk drives?

Don't you need one of these things too? Do you really need two drives? Today's floppy disks come in several flavors. Some PCs use both 5¼-inch

1.2MB and 3½-inch 1.44MB drives, while Macintosh users have standardized on 3½-inch 1.44MB drives. Since most PC software is now being delivered on 3½-inch disks, you really don't need a 5¼-inch drive for your computer. The truth is that as more and more software is being delivered on CD-ROM discs, the floppy disk as we know it may become an endangered species. There is some movement for industry-wide acceptance of Iomega's Zip drive as a floppy replacement, but Compaq Computer, 3M, and Matsushita (Panasonic) are working on a 120MB disk that is backwardly-compatible with 1.44MB floppy disks.

Doing photographic manipulation?

The type of work you use your computer for has an impact on the kind of video display system you need. A display is made up of two components: a monitor and a video board or card. These days, many Mac and PC systems come with video capabilities built into the computer's motherboard. Sometimes you'll need to install a different board in order to make your photographs display on your monitor like "real" photographs and not like pixelized messes. Many inexpensive computers come with an 8-bit color system. While that's adequate for working with black-and-white images, it's barely sufficient for working with and appreciating high-quality color photographs. Only a 16- or 24-bit system will allow you see the nuances of photographs and, more importantly, let you see the effect of any changes you make to these images.

High-quality video boards and color monitors for IBM-compatibles are getting cheaper, but still aren't cheap. Most recent Macintosh models have internal VRAM slots that will accept video SIMMs to increase the visual quality of the display. Take my advice and make sure you have at least 16-bit video. Trying to cut corners with your hardware could result in some unpleasant surprises later, and might cause you to make mistakes when you output an image to film or any other high-resolution presentation.

Getting involved with Photo CD?

I strongly recommend you get involved with Kodak's Photo CD, and if you do, you're going to need a CD-ROM drive to access the on-disc images. Unlike video display hardware, CD-ROM drives are plentiful and inexpensive. They come in both internal and external versions. I have an internal drive in both my PC and Mac because they save desktop space, but either version works fine. Since a CD-ROM disc can hold over 600MB of data on its shiny, plastic surface, this kind of disc can be used for many different kinds of software, especially multimedia.

If you are serious about Photo CD, I strongly recommend that you get a CD-ROM changer. Much like the audio CD changers available for home use, the CD-ROM changer lets you keep five to seven discs on line at one time. Some drives, like the Pioneer changer, even use the same cartridges that are used to hold music CDs. Others, like the inexpensive NEC drives, don't use cartridges.

Working with a service bureau?

There are several considerations here: Is your data portable? Should it be? What quality of output do you want? Besides your hard disk, I strongly suggest you add a removable media drive to your computer system. Drives, like Iomega's Zip, are similar to the hard disk inside your computer, but the disk itself is encapsulated in a plastic shell, making it removable. Iomega Zip drives and cartridges are found in 20 and 100MB capacities, and 1GB Jaz-series drive sizes are also available. For day-to-day use on my Macintosh, I keep a 100MB Zip drive online at all times, with a cartridge I call "Basics" installed. I created another cartridge labeled "Photography" and installed all my Photo CD and image enhancement programs on it. That way, when I want to work with photographs, all of the related programs are available at the same time. If I create an image or series of images with these programs, I copy them temporarily onto my hard disk and insert another cartridge that I take to my photo lab for imaging. If you have a computer in a home office as well as your studio, a removable media drive makes it possible to bring work home by slipping a cartridge into your briefcase instead of carrying an external hard disk back and forth to the studio.

Doing imaging or publishing from the desktop?

You're going to need a good printer. Laser printers lay down a series of dots that are so small that they blend together to form a smooth image. Inside the printer, a tightly focused laser beam scans the image sent to it from the computer, and traces a horizontal line on a light-sensitive, rotating drum. The drum's rotation brings the portion already etched by the laser into contact with the toner. Toner is electrically charged so that it sticks to the dots etched by the laser and is transferred from the drum onto paper.

The quality you get from any printer, including laser printers, depends on the resolution. Printer resolution is measured in dots per inch and the more dots, the better the image looks. At a minimum this should be 300 dpi. Imagesetters, unlike printers, have a resolution of 1,200 dpi to create excellent quality output. Most of these units are too expensive for the average studio, but many service bureaus will provide 1,200 dpi output for a very small charge.

My rule of thumb is to always get the best (most expensive) printer your budget allows, but don't be embarrassed if all you can afford is an inkjet printer, like Epson's family of Stylus Color printers. Instead of using a laser and photo-sensitive drum, an inkjet printer sprays tiny streams of quick-drying ink onto paper. Circuits in the printer turn these little nozzles off and on so the printer forms the same kind of dot pattern that a laser printer does. Inkjet printers are quiet, do an impressive job, and are always cheaper than laser printers—especially color laser printers.

Do you need to fax material to clients?

One last recommendation and I'll be finished spending your money. Get a fax/modem. These clever peripherals allow you to send and receive faxes directly from your desktop. Some low-end products are selling for less than $100, so a fax/modem can pay for itself in a short time. The modem will allow your computer to connect to the Internet, other computers, and to on-line databases. (Think of on-line databases as electronic libraries, but they are more interactive than a traditional library.) Services like CompuServe, America Online, and Prodigy provide electronic mail and sections (called forums) where you can exchange information with other computer users and photographers, as well as providing access to the Information Highway. CompuServe, for instance, has active photography and photojournalism forums. These sections are predominantly PC-oriented, but CompuServe has an extremely active group of Mac-oriented forums.

How much will all this cost?

Whatever you do, don't go into heavy debt on any of these suggestions. Start with a basic box that contains a current generation microprocessor such as a 486 PC or 68040 chip Macintosh. If you can afford the new Pentium or PowerPC chip machines, go for it, because nothing gets in the way of productivity more than a slow computer.

After you've gotten familiar with your system, that's the time to add RAM, larger hard disks, removable media drives, a fax/modem, and other "necessities" as time and budget permits.

There is a myth that the only way digital photographers can create striking images is by owning and using the newest, hottest computer systems. This myth is perpetuated by colorful advertisements and glossy brochures from manufacturers extolling the virtues, speed, and features of their latest boxes. Worse yet, newcomers to digital imaging stand on the sidelines and watch as digital dilettantes purchase these computers in a hopeless quest to replace skill and creativity with hardware. The truth is that even if you purchase the best, most expensive new computer available for digital imaging, there's a good chance that within a few months it will be replaced with one that's better and cheaper. Some people may run after digital nirvana and continue to chase newer and better computers, but does that mean you have to "deep six" your existing computer? Far from it. A used computer can be an excellent bargain for budget-conscious shoppers.

You probably already know that a used camera can be a good buy. That's especially true if the previous owner only used their Hasselblad to take vacation pictures and switched to a Sony camcorder. If the previous owner photographed kids in a high-volume operation and ran four hundred rolls of film a week through their Mamiya RB-67, it might not be such a good idea. Unlike automobiles, computers require only a modest amount of maintenance and often are not used very much. Since silicon chips don't wear out with use, a used computer works the same as a new one. The major "wear and tear" items on a computer are its floppy disk drives and power supply, and you don't have to win the lottery to replace either one.

The ongoing avalanche of new computer models means there are bargains to be found in recently discontinued models. If you can live with the fact that you don't have the latest gee-whiz model the computer magazines are drooling over, chances are a used machine can give excellent service and save you big bucks. Price guides are available to help the used-computer shopper discover what specific models cost. In the back of cross-platform publications, like *ComputerUSER*, you'll find a listing of the National Computer Exchange's (NACOMEX) used-computer prices. Magazines like *MacWorld* publish similar listings from the American Computer Exchange (AMCOMEX).

Armed with prices from the exchanges you'll know how much to pay for the computer of your choice. There are three basic places to look for used computers. The first is the classified ads of your local newspaper. Although some sellers have inflated ideas of what their computers are worth, this is still the best place to find bargains. The equipment may be for sale because the owner needs cash, or perhaps they bought it intending to use it and discovered that computers are not as easy to use as salespeople pretend they are. Either reason can result in a good buy.

An alternative is one of the used-computer stores that are springing up in cities all over the country, but be prepared to pay slightly higher prices. Most dealers offer some kind of guarantee, which can be a significant advantage over buying a computer from someone you discovered in the classifieds. Most used-computer stores I've visited have been staffed with knowledgeable, friendly people, but when buying any used item, *caveat emptor* is always called for. Local conditions can lead to higher or lower prices than the exchanges list.

There are ways for you to protect yourself from buying a lemon instead of an Apple. When buying a used car, it's a good idea to have an expert inspect the car to make sure there are no hidden flaws. That same concept can be applied to shopping for a computer, but here your expert will be software. By using diagnostic programs, such as Win Sleuth Gold Plus for Windows and MacEKG for Macintosh computers, you can check if a computer is in good shape before shelling out your hard-earned cash.

Micromat's MacEKG compiles baseline data and uses it for comparison in subsequent tests. MacEKG factors these results into a system average, and if parameters fall below a user-specified percentage, a message appears suggesting which hardware/software item has decreased performance. MacEKG's logic test calculates eight mathematical formulas and times your Mac to see how fast it performs each one. Component tests look at your computer's five most important integrated circuits and verify if each is operational. Another test scrutinizes Random Access Memory before system software loads and after. The PRAM test performs a series of twenty-five time calculations using Apple's Parameter RAM chip. There are also tests for abnormalities in functionality and performance in both internal and external video. MacEKG tests all read-capable devices on the SCSI bus, and when finished, a histogram chart plots the results and displays a composite performance rating. If you're in trouble, MacEKG issues a warning. When that happens, the screen displays an error code along with Micromat's telephone support number.

Win Sleuth Gold Plus from E-Ware displays a user-configurable graphic of your system along with a tool bar containing buttons for testing System, Environment, Disk, Video, Memory Ports, and Install. After selecting a test, there are more buttons. The Disk screen, for instance, includes buttons for Disk Info, BIOS disks, Disk Partitions, Utilization, and Benchmark. Clicking Benchmark or Utilization causes a Run Test button to appear, and clicking that runs the tests. A new hard disk did well in the random access and full stroke access tests, but under-performed on comparable drives in track-track access. This suggests a problem with the drive—or perhaps the drive wasn't as good as the guy who sold it to me claimed it was.

Win Sleuth's toolbar editors let you access your AUTOEXEC.BAT, CONFIG.SYS, and INI files. I've always regarded these files as the bailiwick of true PC mavens, but Win Sleuth Gold Plus's TuneUp feature gives anyone the tools necessary to make improvements in the way their system software performs. Win Sleuth Gold Plus includes an easy-to-read manual, and traditional Help is also available through the F1 key.

Both programs have been designed to examine hardware components for problems with the computer's logic (mother) board, memory, hard disk, video display, and ports. And neither package is throwaway software. Having diagnostic software in your library can be useful after you've purchased the computer too. One last word: If the person selling the equipment won't let you run one of these programs on the computer they're trying to sell, say "thank you" and move on.

appendix B

Companies Mentioned in This Book

Adobe Systems Inc., 1585 Charleston Road, P.O. Box 7900, Mountain View, CA 94039-7900; 415/961-4400

Alien Skin Software, 2522 Clark Avenue, Raleigh, NC 27607-7214; 919/832-4124, fax: 919/832-4065

AGFA, 200 Ballardvale Street, Wilmington, MA 01887-1069

Apple Computer, 1 Infinite Loop, Cupertino, CA 95014; 408/996-1010

AXS, Marina Village Parkway, Alameda, CA 94501; 510/814-7200, fax: 510/814-6100

Berkeley Systems, 2095 Rose Street, Berkeley, CA 94709; 510/540-5535, fax: 510/540-5630

Bron Imaging Systems, 17 Progress Street, Edison, NJ 08820; 908/754-5800, fax: 908/754-0203

Caere Corporation, 100 Cooper Court, Los Gatos, CA 95030; 800/535-SCAN

Canon Computer Systems, 2995 Redhill Avenue, Costa Mesa, CA 92626; 714/438-3000, fax: 714/438-3099

Canto Software, 800 Duboce Avenue, #101, San Francisco, CA 94117; 415/431-6871, fax: 415/861-6827

Cies-Sexton Photographic Imaging, 1247 Santa Fe Drive, Denver, CO 80204; 303/534-4000, fax: 303/534-4064

Colorado Memory Systems Inc., a division of Hewlett-Packard, 800 S. Taft Avenue, Loveland, CO 80537; 970/669-8000, fax: 970/667-0997

Connectix Corp., 2655 Campus Drive, San Mateo, CA 94403; 415/571-5100, fax: 415/571-5195

Corel Corporation, The Corel Building, 1600 Carling Avenue, Ottawa, Ontario, Canada K1Z8R7; 613/728-8200, fax: 613/728-9790

DataViz, 55 Corporate Drive, Trumbull, CT 06111; 800/733-0030, fax: 203/268-4345

DeltaPoint, 2 Harris Court, Suite B-1, Monterey, CA 93940; 408/648-4000, fax: 408/648-4020

Delta Tao Software, 760 Harvard Avenue, Sunnyvale, CA 94087; 408/730-9336

Deneba Software, 7400 S.W. 87th Avenue, Miami, FL 33173; 305/596-5644, fax: 305/273-9069

Dicomed Inc., 12270 Nicollet Avenue, Burnsville, MN 55337; 612/895-3000, fax: 612/895-3258

Digimation Corporation, 1 Cate Street, Eldredge Park-Portsmouth, NH 03801

Digital Vision, Inc., 270 Bridge Street, Dedham, MA 02026; 617/329-5400

Dycam, 9588 Topanga Canyon Boulevard, Chatsworth, CA 91311; 818/407-3960, fax: 818/407-3966

Eastman Kodak Company, 901 Elmgrove Road, Rochester, NY 14653-5200; 800/235-6325

Educorp Computer Services, 7434 Trade Street, San Diego, CA 92121; 619/536-9999

Envisions Solutions Technology, Inc., 822 Mahler Road, Burlingame, CA 94010; 415/692-9061, fax: 415/692-9064

Epson America Inc., 20770 Madrona Avenue, Torrance, CA 90503; 310/782-0770

Equilibrium Technologies, 475 Gate Five Road, Suite 225, Sausalito, CA 94965; 415/332-4343, fax: 415/332-4433

E-Ware, a division of Visual Cybernetics, 5241 Lincoln Ave, Suite B5, Cypress, CA 90630; 714/236-1380, fax: 714/236-1390

Expert Software, 800 S. Douglas Road, North Tower 355, Coral Gables, FL 33134-3128; 305/567-9990

Fargo Electronics Inc., 7901 Flying Cloud Drive, Eden Prairie, MN 55344; 612/941-9470

Fractal Design Corporation, 510 Lighthouse, Suite 5, Pacific Grove, CA 93950; 408/655-8800

Fuji Photo Film USA Inc., 555 Taxter Road, Elmsford, NY 10523; 800/755-3854, ext. 8253

Halcyon Software, 1590 LaPradera Drive, Campbell, CA 95008; 408/378-9898, fax: 408/378-9935

HSC Software, 6303 Carpinteria Avenue, Carpinteria, CA 93013; 805/566-6200, fax: 805/566-6274

ImageWare Software, Inc., 4330 La Jolla Village Drive, Suite 270, San Diego, CA 92122; 619/457-8600

Imspace Systems Corp., 4747 Morena Boulevard, Suite 360, San Diego, CA 92117; 800/488-KUDO, fax: 619/272-4292

Inner Media Inc., 60 Plain Road, Hollis, NH 03049; 800/962-2949, fax: 603/465-7195

Inset Systems, 71 Commerce Drive, Brookfield, CT 06804-3405; 800/374-6738, fax: 203/775-5634

Insignia Solutions, 2200 Lawson Lane, Santa Clara, CA 95054; 408/327-6000, fax: 408/327-6103

Iomega Corporation, 1821 West Iomega Way, Roy, UT 84067; 800/777-6654, fax: 801/778-3190

JASC Inc., 10901 Red Circle Drive, Suite 340, Minnetonka, MN 55343; 612/930-9171, fax: 612/930-9172

Leaf Systems, 250 Turnpike Road, Southboro, MA 01772-1742; *Digital camera products are marketed and distributed by Sinar.*

Logitech, Inc., 6505 Kaiser Drive, Fremont, CA 94555; 510/795-8500

Media Cybernetics, 8484 Georgia Avenue, Silver Spring, MD 20910; 301/495-3305

Micrografx, 1303 E. Arapaho, Richardson, TX 75081; 800/733-3729, fax: 214/994-6334

Microsoft, One Microsoft Way, Redmond, WA 98052-6399; 800/426-9400

MicroFrontier, Inc., P.O. Box 71190, Des Moines, IA 50325; 515/270-8109

Micromat Computer Systems, 7075 Redwood Boulevard, Novato, CA 94945; 415/898-6227, fax: 415/897-3901

Microtek Lab, Inc., 3715 Doolittle Drive, Redondo Beach, CA 90278; 310/297-5000

Mirror Technologies, 5198 West 76th Street, Edina, MN 55439; 800/643-3384

The MultiMedia Store, 5347 Dietrich Road, San Antonio, TX 78219-2997; 800/597-FOTO

NEC Technologies, Inc., 1255 Michael Drive, Wood Dale, IL 60191-1094

Nikon Electronic Imaging, 1300 Walt Whitman Road, Melville, NY 11747-3064; 516/547-4200

Orange Micro, 1400 N. Lakeview Avenue, Anaheim, CA 92807; 714/779-2772

Play Inc., 2890 Kilgore Road, Rancho Cordova, CA 95670-6153; 800/306-PLAY, fax: 916/851-0801

Pacific Micro, 201 San Antonio Circle, Mountain View, CA 94040; 415/948-6200, fax: 415/948-6296

PhotoPhase Inc., 805 Veterans Boulevard, Suite 200, Redwood City, CA 94063; 415/599-9087; fax: 415/365-0450

Pinnacle Micro, 19 Technology, Irvine, CA 92718; 800/553-7070

Polaroid Corporation, 565 Technology Square, Cambridge, MA 02139; 800/343-5000, fax: 617/386-9339

Primax Electronics, 254 East Hacienda Avenue, Campbell, CA 95008; 800/338-3693

Reply Corporation, 4435 Fortran Drive, San Jose, CA 95134; 800/801-6898

Ricoh Corporation, 3001 Orchard Parkway, San Jose, CA 95134; 408/954-5326, fax: 408/432-9266

Seattle FilmWorks, 1260 16th Avenue West, Seattle, WA 98119-3401; 800/445-3348

Second Glance Software, 25381-G Alicia Parkway, Suite 357, Laguna Hills, CA 92653; 714/855-2331, fax: 714/586-0930

Sony Electronics, 1 Sony Drive, Park Ridge, NJ 07656; 800/352-7669, fax: 408/943-0740

Storm Software, 1861 Landings Drive, Mountain View, CA 94043; 415/691-6600, fax: 415/691-6689

Symantec Corporation, 175 W. Broadway, Eugene, OR 97401-3003; 503/345-3322, fax: 503/334-7488

SyQuest, 47071 Bayside Parkway, Fremont, CA 94538; 510/226-4000

Thunderware, 21 Orinda Way, Orinda, CA 94563-2565; 510/254-6581, fax: 510/254-3407

Ultima International, 3358 Gateway Boulevard, Fremont, CA 94538; 510/659-1580, fax: 510/440-1217

Ulead Systems, 970 West 190th Street, Suite 520, Torrance, CA 90502; 310/523-9393, fax: 310/523-9399

UMAX Technologies, 3353 Gateway Boulevard, Fremont, CA 94538; 510/651-8883

Xaos Tools, 600 Townsend Street, Suite 270 East, San Francisco, CA 94103; 415/487-7000, fax: 415/558-9886

Zoom Telephonics, Inc., 207 South Street, Boston, MA 02111; 800/631-3116, 617/423-1072, fax: 617/423-9231

Allworth Books

Allworth Press publishes quality books to help individuals and small businesses. Titles include:

The Photographer's Internet Handbook by Joe Farace
(softcover, 6 × 9, 208 pages, $18.95)

Arts and the Internet: A Guide to the Revolution by V. A. Shiva
(softcover, 6 × 9, 208 pages, $18.95)

The Internet Publicity Guide by V. A. Shiva
(softcover, 6 × 9, 208 pages, $18.95)

The Photographer's Guide to Marketing and Self-Promotion by Maria Piscopo
(softcover, 6¾ × 10, 176 pages, $18.95)

The Law (in Plain English)® for Photographers by Leonard DuBoff
(softcover, 6 × 9, 208 pages, $18.95)

Business and Legal Forms for Photographers by Tad Crawford
(softcover, 8½ × 11, 192 pages, $16.95)

Pricing Photography by Michal Heron and David MacTavish
(softcover, 11 × 8½, 128 pages, $19.95)

How to Shoot Stock Photos That Sell, Revised Edition by Michal Heron
(softcover, 8 × 10, 208 pages, $19.95)

The Business of Multimedia by Nina Schuyler
(softcover, 6 × 9, 240 pages, $19.95)

The New Business of Design by the International Design Conference in Aspen
(softcover, 6 × 9, 256 pages, $19.95)

Electronic Design and Publishing: Business Practices, Second Edition
by Liane Sebastian (softcover, 6¾ × 10, 216 pages, $19.95)

Licensing Art and Design, Revised Edition by Caryn R. Leland
(softcover, 6 × 9, 128 pages, $16.95)

Please write to request our free catalog. If you wish to order a book, send your check or money order to Allworth Press, 10 East 23rd Street, Suite 400, New York, NY 10010. Include $5 for shipping and handling for the first book ordered and $1 for each additional book. Ten dollars plus $1 for each additional book if ordering from Canada. New York State residents must add sales tax.

If you wish to see our catalog on the World Wide Web, you can find us at Millennium Production's Art and Technology Web site:

http://www.arts-online.com/allworth/home.html
or at **http://www.interport.net/~allworth**